Twayne's English Authors Series

Sylvia E. Bowman, *Editor*

INDIANA UNIVERSITY

Aldous Huxley

 79

Aldous Huxley

By HAROLD H. WATTS

Purdue University

TWAYNE PUBLISHERS

A DIVISION OF G. K. HALL & CO., BOSTON

Contents

Preface

The popular reputation of an author sometimes points to his permanent reputation. In other instances, such a reputation has to undergo a process of rectification, and the esteem and censure of the writer's own time must be modified. With Aldous Huxley it seems likely that much that his own time valued highly, in terms of popularity and comment, is indeed a collection of indications of what later judgment will find in the abundant body of his work.

In his early work Huxley produced novels and essays which gave expression to characteristic modes of early twentieth-century sensibility. Thus, any discussion of representative attitudes of the 1920's can profitably take into account novels like *Crome Yellow* and *Point Counter Point* and the utopian vision of *Brave New World*. The 1920's and the early 1930's were periods in which popular, enlightened estimate of the human situation attempted a work of correction; convictions that to many persons in earlier generations had seemed certain revealed themselves as imperfect and subject to reshaping. Fixed views of sexual morals were discovered to be hypocritical and unrealistic, and the faith held by previous generations concerning scientific discovery and technological progress began to show flaws. Dissatisfaction with accepted ideas accumulated—a dissatisfaction that easily found a mirroring in the satirical novels and the expository prose of the Huxley of the 1920's.

As the work of emancipation revealed itself as incomplete in the 1930's and onwards, public consensus and the insights in the work of the later Huxley began to part company. A certain querulous note commenced to sound in novels like *Eyeless in Gaza* and in expository prose like *Ends and Means*. Earlier works had cleared the intellectual scene of detritus that was a barrier to works of reconstruction, but such later work of Huxley's hardly suited the needs of times when Fascism and Communism threatened the safety of mankind. While Huxley's popularity continued and he was always able to command a large public, considered criticism often chose to regard him as a lost leader who was conducting his continuing public into blind alleys; the trenchant censure of human delusion was giving way to unrealistic views of human possibilities.

The main question to be raised about Huxley's work appears to be: To what extent was Huxley's later effort a turning-aside from effects he first achieved? But it must, in justice to Huxley, be pointed out that the directions he later took do not amount to a clean break with the abilities which first won him his great popular following. He may indeed have betrayed the expectations that early works aroused, but he was not disloyal to the weather-flags already hoisted in them.

To the detection and tracing of these intensifying currents of thought this study of the works of Huxley is devoted. Because such a study has necessarily to be selective, this one neglects a consideration of Huxley's early poetic work and cannot hope to deal specifically with large areas of Huxley's writing for periodicals. It seeks to establish the main tendencies of thought expressed in Huxley's early fiction; it detects characteristic habits of thought and expression announced in the writing that comes to a kind of peak in *Brave New World*. It endeavors, from that point onward, to display the deepening of those habits in work which caused dismay and impatience in many quarters.

Only when such an outline is established is one in a position to estimate, as in the conclusion of this study, the permanent value and interest of Huxley as a writer. How "serious" a writer was Huxley? What claim does he have, in a body of work astoundingly large and often quite repetitious, to represent twentieth-century experience? To what uses can later historians of our time put his abundance?

These are questions to which a survey such as this may offer some answers; but it may also offer answers to other questions that are not just coincidental. How good a novelist was Huxley? What is the relation between the explicit ideas which command a writer's attention and the imaginative works in which they are sometimes embodied? These are problems inextricably linked with the intellectual history of an author who put his hand to many tasks.

Preface

The comparative brevity of this study has imposed certain limitations of treatment. The main lines of Huxley's development are indeed followed; Huxley's abilities as an essayist can be observed in the analysis of *Grey Eminence* and *The Devils of Loudun,* and the general pattern of his intellectual development is offered, of course, in Chapter Two, "The Mind of Aldous Huxley." But the sheer range of Huxley's curiosities and the ingenuity with which they are pursued could be developed only in a larger volume than this one can be. Travel, art criticism, comment on cultural relativities, and a detailed study of style—these are all lines of interest that deserve thorough investigation in relation to the sort of inclusive account offered here.

HAROLD H. WATTS

Purdue University

Chronology

1894 July 6, Aldous Leonard Huxley born, Godalming, Surrey, son of Leonard and Judith (Arnold). (Older brother Julian born June 22, 1887.)

1903 Attendance at Hillside School, near Godalming, Surrey.

1905 Journey to Lake Country with parents.

1908 Enters Eton; death of mother. Eton education ended by blindness; made a partial recovery in his days at Oxford.

1913 Enters Balliol College, Oxford.

1914 Suicide of brother Trev.

1915 First participation in the circle of literary persons at Garsington Manor House under the sponsorship of Lady Ottoline Morrell; acquaintance with T. S. Eliot, Osbert Sitwell, J. M. Murry, and others. First meeting with D. H. Lawrence in London.

1916 Publication of *The Burning Wheel*, first volume of poems. Short story, "Eupompus Gave Splendour to Art by Numbers," published in the *Palatine Review*. Brief period of farm-work.

1917 Work in the War Office; teacher at Eton.

1919 Marriage with Belgian refugee, Maria Nys. Start of journalistic career with the *London Athenaeum;* articles and reviews under the pseudonym of Autolycus.

1920– Drama critic of *Westminster Gazette*. Birth of son Mat-
1921 thew.

1921 First novel, *Crome Yellow*.

1922 Collection of stories, *Mortal Coils*.

1923 *Antic Hay*. Transfer of residence to the Continent.

1925 *Those Barren Leaves*.

1925– World travel; material gathered for *Jesting Pilate* (1926).
1926

1926 Renewal of friendship with D. H. Lawrence.

1928 *Point Counter Point.*

1929 Collection of essays, *Do What You Will.*

1930 Censorship of *Brief Candles* by Irish Free State Censorship Board. Death of D. H. Lawrence, whose letters Huxley edits in 1932. Purchase of small house at Sanary near Toulon in southern France.

1931 First acquaintance with the visual methods of Dr. W. H. Bates. First meeting with Gerald Heard.

1932 *Brave New World.*

1934 Travels in Central America and southern Mexico. Travel journal, *Beyond the Mexique Bay.*

1935 Association with the Reverend Dick Sheppard in British Pacifist meetings. First lecture on peace and internationalism. Activity on behalf of German Jews.

1936 *Eyeless in Gaza;* book impounded by Australian Censorship Board.

1937 Transfer of residence to southern California. First association with the Vedanta movement of California and Swami Prabhavananda. *Ends and Means.*

1939 Begins association with Christopher Isherwood. *After Many a Summer Dies the Swan.*

1941 Scenario for *Pride and Prejudice. Grey Eminence.*

1944 Scenario for *Jane Eyre. Time Must Have a Stop.*

1945 *The Perennial Philosophy.*

1948 Successful production of the dramatic version of the short story, "The Gioconda Smile"; produced as a film, *A Woman's Vengeance. Ape and Essence.*

1950 Collection of essays, *Themes and Variations.*

1952 *The Devils of Loudun.*

1953 Association with Humphry Osmund; experiment with psychedelic drugs recorded in *The Doors of Perception* (1954).

1955 Death of first wife. Publication of *The Genius and the Goddess.*

1956 Marriage with Laura Archera. Collection of essays, *Tomorrow and Tomorrow and Tomorrow* (English title: *Adonis and the Alphabet*).

1958 Publication of *Brave New World Revisited,* commentary on *Brave New World.*

1959 Award from the American Academy of Letters.

1960 Huxley's cancer of the tongue diagnosed.

Chronology

1961   Burning of California residence in a brush fire; destruction of papers. Trips to a literary congress in India and to Brazil, and Europe.

1962   Elected a Companion of Literature of the British Royal Society of Literature (one of ten such positions). *Island.*

1963   Participation in the drafting of a program on Human Possibilities for the World Academy in Stockholm. Continuing activity as a lecturer. Death in California, November 22.

CHAPTER 1

Biographical

A SHORT time after the death of Aldous Huxley on November 22, 1963, a collection of memorial essays appeared, *Aldous Huxley, 1894–1963*.[1] In this collection edited by Huxley's famous brother, biologist Julian Huxley, are included papers read at a memorial meeting in London and tributes offered by Aldous Huxley's friends throughout the world: writers, musicians, educators, and scientists. Other material from which knowledge of the biographical details of Huxley's career can be drawn comes from the memoirs and biographies of persons with whom Huxley was in contact in the years of unremitting literary activity that extended from his first volume of poems, *The Burning Wheel* (1916), to his last book, *Literature and Science* (1963).

The main outlines of that career are clear enough: Huxley supported himself by his literary endeavors over a span of more than forty-five years with works that included novels, essays, poetry, biographies, cultural analyses, and unabashed "tracts for the times." Though there are a good many other figures in the first half of the twentieth century, Huxley has some claim to be regarded as an example of Carlyle's "hero as a literary man." The age of the hero as inspired prophet, at any rate, has perhaps departed. Nevertheless, the storms of the twentieth century have been "ridden" by many meditative and concerned writers such as François Mauriac and Thomas Mann.

These are men who have found that their literary careers involved them in at least a double obligation: to chart the actual direction and force of the "winds of doctrine" turbulent in their day, and to modify—with whatever authority and freedom they were able to exercise because of their writing and reputations—the directions in which those winds blew. This action was often taken at considerable risk to their critical reputations, as the experience of Huxley indicates. For Huxley wrote in a time when literary distinction was judged by canons of taste that were suspicious of writing that, like his, involved itself directly in the turbulence and change of a century and that tried to indicate channels for awesome forces.

In fiction, for example, the model of Gustave Flaubert suggested that the most perfect works of art were formed by creators who avoided merging artistic concerns with social, political, and moral problems.[2] Huxley—particularly during the last two-thirds of his career—did not hesitate to regard whatever he wrote as a possible contribution to the clarification of his turbulent century. He did not stand apart from it to create works of art esthetically self-sufficient. Instead, with a readiness that some would regard as heroic and others as indiscreet, he involved himself and his works in some of the main problems of his time.

As a result, he learned as much as he could (often a great deal) of the scientific thought of his day. He also achieved an impressive mastery of sections of the human past, not for its own sake but for what older temporary solutions of human problems might have to contribute to contemporary solution. He played, in turn and often in the same novel or essay, the role of sociologist and philosopher; he did not hesitate, in his later years, to assume the outmoded role of prophet. Huxley's body of work makes clear that he regarded the writer as a person who should be, in current phraseology, an involved or committed man.

One way to suggest the variety of Huxley's involvements and commitments is to observe the range of contacts he formed over his long life. If one were to compose a work entitled "Aldous Huxley and His Circle," one would display a man whose interests took him into many circles. He had, to be sure, the "literary friendships" that are the result of celebrity and success; the presently available records suggest contacts, friendly and sometimes close, with D. H. Lawrence, Virginia Woolf, T. S. Eliot, Osbert Sitwell, and a good many others. But, as the list of the contributors to the memorial volume suggests, Huxley's wide-ranging and (to him) necessary curiosities led him to form friendships with scientists, sociologists, and propagandists for the advance of man.

As the memorial essays make quite clear, persons were drawn to Huxley for a variety of reasons. It is not easy to imagine for Huxley such meetings of friends as Dr. Samuel Johnson presided over in eighteenth-century London; nor is it easy to imagine an evening in Los Angeles that would include Greta Garbo; Anita Loos, the author of the once-celebrated *Gentlemen Prefer Blondes*; Gerald Heard, the expositor of the "everlasting gospel"; a scientist like Dr. Humphry Osmond; a molder of public opinion like Robert M. Hutchins; Yehudi Menuhin; and Christopher Isherwood and other Vedantists who immerse themselves (in Alfred Kazin's unkind description) in a West Coast Ganges.

But such persons have recorded the friendship that they enjoyed with him. Moreover, the available testimony speaks with great unanimity of Huxley's kindness, of his lack of animus and envy. It would seem that the fear that haunted Philip Quarles, a kind of *alter ego* of Huxley's in *Point Counter Point*, had little basis in Huxley's actual experience of life. Quarles describes himself as an intellectual isolated from others, from contacts that he realizes he needs badly.[3] Quarles' fears—perhaps expressive of Huxley's estimate about 1928 of his own capacities for establishing human contact—were not realized in Huxley's later life. Whether such fears were contributing elements to Huxley's writing is another matter; they must be dealt with in estimates of Huxley's literary character as opposed to what one may grant about Huxley the man who was, it is clear, an encourager of others and one who esteemed others.

I *The Life and the Work*

In short, the survey one can make of Huxley's life does not suggest that it will ever be very profitable to use the events and patterns of this writer's life as keys that unlock the meaning of the man's great mass of writing. The most that one can predict is that some of the keys would be quite useful; others, not at all. Here is a considerable contrast to what can and must be done with the novels, tales, and poems of Huxley's close friend, D. H. Lawrence, whose social origins, emotional drives, and personal resentments make telling contributions to the works of art. It would, for example, be over-ingenious and somewhat impertinent to take off from the defect of eyesight that plunged Huxley, as a youth, into two years of blindness and to suggest that this experience of isolation begot the solitude that surrounds so many of Huxley's fictional personages. It would, in contrast, be just to trace the contribution that Huxley's upper-class origins made to his sort of literary work—erudite, self-confident, and more than a little condescending. And it would not be difficult to establish the shaping effects of early London friendships.

But such biographical information, one imagines, will often only confirm tendencies and ranges of interest that are quite clear in the writing itself rather than—as much Lawrence criticism suggests—become keys to unlock dark chambers that otherwise resist entrance. Indeed, the even course of Huxley's private life—specifically, his two marriages—suggests that his many records of sexual confusion and more inclusive bitterness did not come to him from any personal disappointments.

II *The Course of Events*

Aldous Huxley was born on July 6, 1894, at Godalming, Surrey. His parents were Leonard Huxley and Judith (Arnold) Huxley. Aldous Huxley was the youngest of three sons; Julian, the celebrated biologist, was his senior by seven years. (A middle brother, Trev, committed suicide in 1914.) Aldous Huxley's full christening name was Aldous Leonard Huxley; he early dropped the second name, which, it may be noted, was his father's name.

Future scholars may be able to determine whether the relation of Huxley to his parents was any model for the pattern of child-parent relationship which is rather normal in Huxley's fictions: one more marked by antagonism than respect and affection. It is sufficient to note here that Huxley's parents were persons of much distinction in their own right. Leonard Huxley was educated as a Classics scholar and was, from 1901 onwards, editor of the *Cornhill Magazine;* he was also engaged in other literary tasks such as editions of the letters of T. H. Huxley, Jane Welsh Carlyle, and Elizabeth Barrett Browning. Mrs. Huxley was the founder of a girls' school.[4] Her early death in 1908 was a shock, both deep and understandable, to her son; and the void she left was not successfully filled by Leonard Huxley's second wife.[5]

Through his two parents, Huxley had a distinguished ancestry. His paternal grandfather, Thomas Henry Huxley, the champion of Charles Darwin and his theories,[6] was a model of devotion to the pursuit of sober investigation wherever it led, and yet a stern moralist who could advocate the study of the Bible in the schools.[7] Huxley's mother was a grand-niece of Matthew Arnold, also a kind of model of certain Victorian tendencies: concern with the discovery and cherishing of moral seriousness; concern—perhaps deeper than Thomas Henry Huxley's—with the implications for conduct of accumulating scientific insight. For Arnold had heard with dismay, on Dover beach, the retreat of the "sea of faith" that had supported and directed human consciousness for many centuries past; his somewhat prophetic insight allowed him to look forward to times when Classical studies and biblical piety would both have disappeared from English culture. (Through his mother, Huxley was also related to Mrs. Humphrey Ward, a novelist celebrated in her own day for sober treatments of questions disturbing the minds of her contemporaries.)

Viewing this combined inheritance, one is tempted to construct a neat paradigm to describe the two famous sons of Leonard and Julia Huxley: Julian worked out many of the implications of the confidence that his grandfather, Thomas Henry Huxley, had in the enlightenment that comes from scientific studies; and Aldous, intermittently sensitive to the dismay that came to his other ancestor, Matthew Arnold, was, in the latter portions of his career, determined to find substitutes for the healing that the "sea of faith" once offered mankind. But it is only just to note that Julian Huxley has labored outside the laboratory and has been as deeply concerned as his novelist brother for the good estate of man. Moreover, Aldous Huxley opened many a laboratory door at stages in his quest for surrogates to the ancient effects of the "sea of faith." The two brothers, whatever their theoretical differences —stemming chiefly from contrasting estimates of what man is— could join forces in their mature years in support of causes they mutually approved.[8]

At the age of nine, Aldous Huxley was, like most English boys of his class, sent off to a preparatory school—to Hillside School, near Godalming. In the opinion of Huxley's cousin, Gervas Huxley, this school receives unflattering treatment in *Eyeless in Gaza* under the name of Bulstrode[9]—a portrayal not entirely in accord with Gervas' own recollections of the years he had passed there with Aldous. Bulstrode, at least, is marked by snobbery and cruelty and overshadowed by the sexual troubles of young boys.[10] That occasional rays of light fell into this darkness of Huxley's five years at Hillside is indicated by the recollections of others; for Huxley early impressed his peers with his intellectual superiority, and his pleasant vacations with his parents took him to the English lake country and to Switzerland.

After five years at Hillside, Huxley entered Eton (1908), where he endured troubling years. His mother's death was deeply disorienting for him;[11] and, toward the end of his stay, occurred the onset of blindness—keratitis, or irritation of the cornea—that put an end to his hopes for a career in science. All the persons who recall Huxley's response to this challenge express admiration:[12] Huxley taught himself Braille and praised the benefits of that skill for a boy who wished to continue to read after dormitory lights were extinguished. He also learned to type and composed a novel which he was never able to read because he lost the manuscript before the partial return of vision. An additional solace to him was his considerable ability on the piano.

From Eton, still in the company of his cousin Gervas, Huxley went to Balliol College at Oxford. In the course of his first year there, he had the happiness of recovering partial use of his sight although for many years he could read only with the aid of various sorts of glasses. (It was the wonder of later acquaintances that Huxley, handicapped as he was, was able to respond to so much in the works of art he constantly sought out.[13]) Whatever his private troubles—concern with his sight, uneasiness over his inability to share in the war experiences of his young relatives and friends—the Huxley of Oxford impressed others deeply as a young man confident in his emerging intellectual powers, always ready for elaborate discourse and sometimes for conversation, eager to take part in amateur theatricals, and pleased to contribute to the literary life of the University.[14]

At this time Huxley already possessed the ready and curious erudition that—a frequent gibe—was drawn from the *Encyclopaedia Britannica* but certainly came from other sources as well. Later, in 1925, one of Huxley's preparations for a tour of the world was packing a set of the *Britannica* to travel with him.[15] And a visitor to his household in the south of France in the 1930's recalls the presence of the *Britannica* on the shelves there.[16] But Huxley's mind was more than encyclopedic; curious information was esteemed not for its own sake but for the uses to which it could be put. Huxley was also, by the time of his Oxford years, fluent in the French language; his later work is full of indications that he knew the byways as well as the main avenues of Gallic culture. There are also signs of ease with Latin, Italian, Spanish, and German.

During the years at Oxford, Huxley made his first appearances in print, although these had been anticipated at Hillside.[17] His story "Eupompus Gave Splendor to Art by Number" appeared in a short-lived magazine, *The Palatine Review;*[18] and a collection of poetry, *The Burning Wheel,* was published in 1916. Poetry, one should note, was a literary form that Huxley persisted in for the next ten years and then abandoned for fiction and essay—perhaps as a result of a discouraging suggestion from T. S. Eliot.[19] In retrospect, Huxley continued to regard the writing of poetry as a normal activity of the gifted young; the seventeen-year-old Sebastian Barnach in *Time Must Have a Stop* (1945) composes verses —ones strongly resembling those of Huxley.

Huxley had already achieved the physical presence that everyone who knew him remarks on—tall, lean, and, perhaps because of his defect of vision, somewhat Olympian and detached in manner.[20]

Near the end of his Oxford experience, Huxley made an acquaintance that was both defining and practically useful to a young man who wished to enter the literary world; he was introduced to Lady Ottoline Morrell, who presided over a casually assembled circle of the great and the promising at her manor house in Garsington, near Oxford. Lady Ottoline was the determined patroness of such figures as D. H. Lawrence, Lytton Strachey, Bertrand Russell, Katherine Mansfield, and John Middleton Murry;[21] and Huxley easily won a place among these persons. The atmosphere of Garsington was that of free thinking and free speaking; the assemblage was one that was looked on with some suspicion because of its pacifist and other opinions, as the novelist Naomi Mitchison recalls—*she* was forbidden by her conventional parents to join it.[22] Toward the end of World War I, Huxley joined other members of the group in agricultural labors which diminished his sense of uneasiness at being a non-combatant. But Garsington was important for him primarily because it gave him a view of the stimulating literary world which he hoped to enter; there is considerable agreement that Lady Ottoline's household was the model for the country house life that is represented in his first novel, *Crome Yellow* (1921).[23] It was an atmosphere full of scorn for the smug and one that often cradled hopes for a freer, wiser use of human opportunity.[24]

Upon completion of his studies at Oxford—from which he

emerged with an Honors Degree in English literature—Huxley
cast about for some means of support (he was already in love
with a young Belgian refugee named Maria Nys, whom he had
met at Garsington). His first attempt at self-support was teaching
at Eton in 1918; at this task he was neither a notable success nor a
great failure; he was provocative to some of his charges and an
erudite enigma to others.[25] Like Theodore Gumbril in *Antic Hay*
(1923), Huxley retreated to London and soon found openings in
literary journalism. He contributed reviews and articles to the
Athenaeum, edited by John Middleton Murry; some of these,
signed Autolycus in the journal, presently appeared as a first collection of essays, *On the Margin* (1923).[26] Among his other labor
was a stint as the dramatic critic of the *Westminster Gazette* in
1920 and 1921.

Thanks to the degree of security he had attained, Huxley married Maria Nys in the summer of 1919. From this marriage one
son, Matthew, was born. All accounts of the marriage, it is pleasant to note in contrast to the painful representations of love and
marriage in much of Huxley's fiction, agree that it was a successful
one. Mrs. Huxley, far from being a literary person herself, entered
willingly into the activities of her husband; she shared in Huxley's
lengthy travels; she typed his manuscripts and the manuscripts of
his friends; she was a generous hostess in the various places in
Italy, France, and California to which Huxley's wanderings led.[27]

With the appearance of *Crome Yellow* (1921) and *Antic Hay*
(1923), Huxley's reputation was quickly established. These novels, which struck readers as satiric and welcome rejection of the
tedious past which their elders revered, enabled Huxley to abandon his journalism and to move away from the depressing climate
of England to sunnier places, chiefly Italy and France in the
1920's and the early 1930's. It should be noted that Huxley's aban-
donment of formal journalistic employment in London did not
amount to a halt of journalistic effort; the sheer bulk of his work—
produced at the rate of about five hundred words a day, one observer relates[28]—was occasioned by the necessity of meeting the
modest needs of his own household and the sometimes less modest needs of the many persons Huxley was generous to.

By the middle of the 1920's, Huxley's life had achieved a pattern that lasted at least until 1937, when the Huxley's made their

permanent settlement in California. During the 1920's Huxley's journeys through France, Italy, and Spain in a high-powered car[29] and his trip around the world in 1925 and 1926 (recorded in *Jesting Pilate*) do indeed lack much of the passion that D. H. Lawrence was expending on his travels in the same period; Lawrence was forever discovering in ancient Etruscans or in modern Mexican groups a fashion of living that had been missed or lost in "civilized" England. In contrast, Huxley travels with the sense that there is much to learn and to be amused by, wherever one goes. For Huxley, there is almost no sense that one place of instruction—a distant country, a neglected era of the past—is necessarily a better place of instruction; it is certainly not likely to be the only one.

Instead, there is an eager and yet modest expectation that continues throughout Huxley's life: that a journey to Central America (recorded in *Beyond the Mexique Bay* [1934]) or to the Far East (*Adonis and the Alphabet* [1956]; American title: *Tomorrow and Tomorrow and Tomorrow*) will add pieces to the jigsaw on which an ingenious observer is working. One can observe that, even though Huxley lived for more than twenty-five years in southern California, the place was no more his home, in the conventional and perhaps sentimental sense, than some villa near Lucca where he had halted for a short time in the late 1920's. California—like Lucca, or like some Hindu town visited only overnight—remained a place to be inspected, to be interpreted by ironic description and apt cultural parallels.

During his years of chiefly Continental residence, Huxley wrote works that commanded—and command—wide public attention: *Point Counter Point* (1928), *Brave New World* (1932), and others. During his Italian sojourns in the late 1920's he formed his most celebrated friendship: the relation with D. H. Lawrence— that restless traveler who was a seeker for a locus of revelation rather than a cultural tourist like Huxley, who did not expect his travels to conduct him to a goal. Huxley had met Lawrence earlier[30] and rejected Lawrence's suggestion of setting up an ideal colony in Florida. After 1926, however, and to the time of Lawrence's death in 1930 in Vence, Huxley and his wife devoted themselves to the well-being of Lawrence and Frieda, his wife, with singular, self-effacing piety. It was concern that one can see

in Huxley's offer of a car to the Lawrences,[31] in the support that
Huxley gave Lawrence in the disputes about *Lady Chatterley's
Lover*,[32] and in the last weeks of Lawrence's life.[33] A continuing
concern for the reputation of his dead friend was responsible for
an edition of Lawrence's letters which Huxley edited[34]—a collection still basic to present-day Lawrence scholarship. This evidence, as well as the picture of Lawrence drawn in the figure of
Rampion in *Point Counter Point*, suggests that Lawrence's focus
of gesture and aspiration was immensely suggestive to Huxley.

But this focus came by degrees to count less for Huxley in the
troubled 1930's.[35] From Lawrence and Italy, one might say, Huxley's curiosity moved on to other places, works of art, persons,
social experiments, scientific discoveries, and even personal investigations of drugs (LSD) and of hypnotism. Here also were items
that had a right to a place in the intellectual equation that Huxley
was, to the very end of his life, adding to and hoping to balance.

The decade of the 1930's—concluded for most modern imaginations by the descent of the smoky curtain of World War II—was
for Huxley, as the years advanced, a time of restless change of
location, terminated only by his settling in southern California in
1937. To a *New York Times* reporter, Huxley explained: "I
stopped there on my way to India, and because of inertia and
apathy remained." [36] There were stronger motives: the beneficial
effect of the bright light of the region on Huxley's vision and the
accessibility of a center where the techniques of Dr. W. H. Bates
helped Huxley to improve his eyesight.[37] In addition to *Brave
New World* (1932), this decade was marked by two novels, *Eyeless in Gaza* (1936) and *After Many a Summer Dies the Swan*
(1939). Highly significant for Huxley's passage from amused detachment to deep, undisguised concern is the long essay or tract,
Ends and Means (1937), the first of several frontal attacks on a
time notoriously out of joint.

Altering circumstances in Huxley's life are outward signs of his
changed estimate of a writer's function. Like the hero of *Eyeless
in Gaza*. Anthony Beavis, Huxley overcame his repugnance to
public speaking and spoke at rallies on behalf of the peace and
internationalism that, in his judgment, the mass of men were
blind to; he allied his efforts with those of Gerald Heard and the
Reverend Dick Sheppard to curb the insanity that was preparing
men for general slaughter.[38] As he was to do for the rest of his

life, he delivered public lectures of his own to publicize views that he felt were for the general good. He performed acts of deep beneficence, as when, along with his brother Julian, he intervened with the British government, which was about to pass regulations that would make it impossible for English citizens to rescue Jewish women by marrying them.[39]

If one wishes an almost symbolic expression of the change noted here, one can observe that one of the deepest friendships Huxley formed after the death of Lawrence was with Gerald Heard, whom he met in 1931, worked with in public causes, and re-encountered when he took up residence in southern California. Heard was not, like Lawrence, a man who turned aside from social responsibility in the name of winning closer contact with blood or instinct or life-force. He was, instead, a man deeply attentive to the human uses of all the findings of science and sociology and psychology; in fact, his later development in California runs parallel to Huxley's own. It was in California that Heard had already encountered teachers of Eastern wisdom, the Vedanta; and, with another English expatriate, Christopher Isherwood, Heard had pursued the study of the wisdom of India. With this circle—formally known as the Vedanta Society of Southern California—Huxley associated himself.

With mutual encouragement and with the help of Hindu instructors like Krishnamurti and Swami Prabhavananda, the English writers labored to reconcile the West with the East in such works as Heard's *The Eternal Gospel* (1946) and as Huxley's *The Perennial Philosophy* (1945). The work of these English exiles has aroused irritation in many quarters; it is enough to observe at this point that Huxley was perhaps stimulated by Heard's insights and found a clue that sufficed him when the insights of D. H. Lawrence had lost their power to illuminate his mind. Was it a clue that betrayed Huxley's talent? This question must wait upon an inspection of the latter half of Huxley's work; it is not surprising that Christopher Isherwood judges that Huxley's best books were those of the second half of his life.[40]

Shortly after his arrival in California, Huxley gave other signs of his amazing and, to some, disconcerting expertise. Aided by Anita Loos, the author of *Gentlemen Prefer Blondes*, Huxley had the opportunity of writing the film-script of *Pride and Prejudice* in 1941, a remarkably faithful treatment of Jane Austen's novel.[41]

(He was also involved in work on two later films: *Jane Eyre;* a treatment of the life of Madame Curie; and the film version of his successful play, *The Gioconda Smile*—which was given the more sensational title, *A Woman's Vengeance*.[42])

There is little sign that Huxley, in the last twenty-five years of his life, found reason to modify the harsh judgments that he had pronounced on West Coast civilization in *Jesting Pilate* (1926).[43] He could express admiration for the deserts and mountains; he continued the interest in painting which he had taken up many years before in southern France;[44] and he was particularly impressed by the Joshua trees of the California desert.[45] He could also take pleasure in the wide variety of social contacts the Los Angeles area provided for him. (Anita Loos's account of a picnic at which the Huxleys, along with Miss Loos, Greta Garbo, the Hindu teacher Krishnamurti, and others were nearly arrested as vagrants by an angry policeman is an amusing record of the position of the arts in America and has a startling resemblance to incidents that Huxley invented for his fiction.[46]) But Huxley found no reason to question his earlier estimate of the deleterious forms of materialism and pleasure-seeking that continued to be the norms of human action in his place of final residence. An observer has found as rather strange Huxley's indifference to the vulgarity of the furnishings of the house where he lived for many years.[47] Perhaps Huxley's amused tolerance is not unlike that which the sophisticated person offers popular arts; to find them amusing rather than contemptible is proof of one's complex powers of insight.

During his last ten years of life, Huxley aroused attention, some of it unfavorable, by the personal experiments he made, under the careful direction of his friend, Dr. Humphry Osmond, with hallucinogenic drugs;[48] here Huxley found, as he makes clear in *The Doors of Perception* (1954), material aids to the intensification of insight that, supposedly, some of the great visionaries of the past had achieved by themselves. It is just to note that Huxley's interest in drugs, in hypnotism, and in some of the other fringe benefits of existence in California were not random; human reaction was, as Huxley judged the matter, pitiful in its narrowness of range, and the student who was concerned to broaden that range and to intensify its subtlety would investigate all the means that presented themselves.[49]

These interests did not, however, cancel Huxley's concern with the immediate problems which civilization faces. He continued the lecturing he had begun in the late 1930's; he accepted invitations to speak at universities and meetings devoted to such causes as control of hunger and excessive growth of population, and he contributed to schemata useful for the deliberations of international congresses.[50] Like his brother Julian, Huxley was in his last years something of a public figure; various awards and citations underlined the degree of importance he had won.[51]

All the recollections of Huxley's last decade underline the persistence of his kindness, his pursuit of useful information, and his stoic endurance of his own physical sufferings, including the cancer that finally brought about his death. Mrs. Huxley had died of the same disease in 1955. In the year following his wife's death, Huxley married again; his second wife was Laura Archera, an Italian concert violinist.[52] All reports indicate Huxley's courage and resignation when a brush fire destroyed his home and all his papers in 1961; the cancellation of the material detritus of the past was, Huxley indicated, in a way beneficial: it cleared the way to new tasks. This attitude, less strikingly, marks most of Huxley's work: in many books he gives the impression of taking up problems for the first time rather than, as a matter of fact, for the fourth or fifth time.[53]

Huxley's death took place on November 22, 1963—the same day as the assassination of President John Kennedy. The progressive effects of cancer had been working for three years; they had scarcely diminished Huxley's flow of composition and even his continuing travel; and, in the last week of his life, he managed to finish an essay entitled "Shakespeare and Religion."

Such are the outlines of Huxley's life: outlines it is useful to refer to, from time to time, as one undertakes an analysis of his work, various and abundant. It should be clear that there is little of the shocking or the *outré* in his personal behavior or relationships; intellectual boldness and its reflection in prose and spoken argument were, for Huxley, a sufficient repudiation of elements in the past that deformed the present.

CHAPTER 2

The Mind of Aldous Huxley

THE literary career of Aldous Huxley provoked an enthusiastic response. The persistent sale of his books indicates that twentieth-century readers had impressions and malaises that responded to the illumination in Huxley's books like images on undeveloped photographic plates. His essays, his novels, and his utopias (particularly *Brave New World*) were the chemical agents that fixed the images and outlines that were already potential. Huxley's books could be read as an effort to discredit the main features of a dishonest past that ignored crucial elements in human existence. And it is true that Huxley is unremitting in his censure of uncritical faith in the benefits of material and social progress. It is also true that Huxley comes around to a defense of a positive account of human capacities that does not make cancellation in itself an act of sufficient wisdom.

The human being was, according to the Huxley instruction, a creature whose complexity was ignored or simplified by the religion, morality, and facile social hopes that Victorian and Edwardian education had imposed on the young. Hasty judgment of Huxley, resting on early novels like *Crome Yellow* (1921), *Antic Hay* (1923), and *Point Counter Point* (1928), led many readers to judge that destruction and emancipation were identical. A green light flashed in a work like *Point Counter Point,* and the highway it signaled was broad and free of perplexing curves. (The curves on the Huxley freeway appeared later, as shall be seen.)

That discrediting of the past of one's elders is the single act necessary for achievement of a wise freedom—is not an impression that stirred and then died in the 1920's of this century. But Huxley can still be recognized as a writer who is on the right path and thus on the side of the angels that preside over the process of being human in the twentieth century. Indeed, there is much in the later work of Huxley that continues this vein, and a somewhat uncritical reader can judge that he is still in the presence of the old or original Huxley as he reads later books. The habits of the *enfant terrible* persist in works in which Huxley is attempting labors that could not possibly interest a sheerly destructive mind.

Yet a general sketch of the mind of Huxley must indicate that Huxley was, from the early 1930's onward, trying to refound society and the individual human sensibility on a basis that included more than just an omnibus reflection of Victorian and Edwardian convictions. One can say that all that follows *Brave New World* (1932) should often be disturbing to minds which cast Huxley in the simple role of an avenging angel who drives mankind forth from the ersatz Eden which was the Victorian world. The later Huxley is a beneficent—if often captious—angel driving mankind toward a better Eden.

Huxley in the role of an almost angelic reconstructor of shattered human sensibility has startled and disturbed readers; he aroused impatience, incredulity, and even condescension.[1] So long as Huxley was content to speak for an undefinable life-force[2] and for a ready acceptance of undefinable variety in the human self, he could be regarded as speaking for his own time. When, however, he put his talents to the service of emerging convictions of his own (and not just his own, he would add, but convictions linked with a "Perennial Philosophy"), Huxley betrayed the expectations of some of his readers.

Huxley, of course, does not go back to the compromises he had mocked: those that had characterized optimistic Victorian Christianity. Instead, Huxley turns to solutions that Victorian Christianity ignored: in general, a blend of faith in science and devotion to religious insights that are of Eastern rather than Western origin. It is as if Huxley came around to speaking of a promised land, the actual existence of which lies beyond demonstration.

To those who are not moved by Huxley's later convictions, the later hopeful forays on branches of science seem a rejection of the devastating mockery of scientism contained in *Brave New World*. And Huxley's persistent meditation on the role of mystical insight is an about-face and a retreat from earlier presentations of religion as root-and-branch delusion. Does not Huxley end by being the figure of fun that his earlier work pilloried? In *Point Counter Point*, among those who are mocked is Burlap, a literary critic

whose nauseous stock-in-trade is a pseudo-Franciscan spirituality;
at the end of the novel is the famous glimpse of Burlap and his
mistress pretending to be children in their bath—"Of such is the
Kingdom of Heaven." [3] It is an ending that arouses mirth for *all*
of mankind's spiritual pretensions. When, thirty-odd years later,
Huxley places drug-induced vision at the center of the relatively
good society in *Island,* what has overtaken the once-confident satirist? A failure of nerve? Perhaps. But the contrast also records a
publicly executed meditation upon human capacities.

I *The Background*

The intellectual journey conveniently symbolized by the passage from Burlap to Farnaby in *Island* is one that detaches Huxley from the role of iconoclast and casts him in the role of a guru
—a spiritual instructor of his time. As an iconoclast, Huxley was a
challenger of the certainties of the Victorian and Edwardian es-
tablishments in England and of the similar ones that flourished in
the United States during what Joseph Wood Krutch has called the
"age of confidence." As the spiritual instructor that he became,
Huxley lost none of the brashness that went with his earlier
stance; he added positive convictions about human capacities that
once would have aroused his mirth. Why he came to hold these
convictions is best understood by reference to the broad outlines
of shifts in opinion in his time.

In the second decade of this century, the Victorian sunset had
already occurred in a sky full of threatening clouds—clouds that
put in doubt the likelihood that the next day would be as fair as
had been, supposedly, the one that had just ended. The clouds
had long been in the sky. Darwin's challenge to the unique dignity of man was, in Aldous Huxley's youth, already a familiar one.
The implications of the theories of natural selection and mutation
as the causes of diversity in the animal kingdom were already
widely recognized. If the structure of that kingdom expressed not
a divine will but the interplay of physical environment and
chance genetic transformation, then much was put in question.
What of the divine guidance of the universe by a deity who was
both personal and transcendent? If, as much science suggested,
the physical world had been the creation of long geological periods and not the work of six days of divine labor, chance seemed

to be the guide that governed the emergence of both the inanimate and the animate worlds.

It was not only this account of creation that cast shadows on the authority of Holy Scripture and, by implication, on religiously based morality. The Bible itself had been, from 1862 onwards, subjected to the "higher criticism" imported from Germany by Bishop Colenso and others.[4] The Bible was revealed not as the product of divine authorship but as a human fabrication subject to the very kind of critical study already offered the *Iliad* and other great works of the past; like them, it should be regarded as a cultural monument and not as the source of unchanging truth.

Such clouds as these cast shadows on an aspect that, for Huxley, was very central indeed to any scheme of human action. It seemed clear that human values did not have their ultimate origin in the mind and utterance of deity (God's will for man); they had, instead, devious origins in man's will for himself. This generalization might encourage an inclusive respect for all human codes; but what about continued obedience to a particular code, such as the collection of customs and taboos that regulated family relations and public morality? Such a code, T. H. Huxley and Herbert Spencer might argue, was worthy of continuation because it was socially useful; it had contributed to social cohesion, to comfort, and even to prosperity and progress. But confidence in a particular code was open to skeptical question as soon as wide-ranging study increased the knowledge of the varying codes observed by non-Western portions of the human race. (It was ironical that one of the most influential of these investigations was made by an Anglican bishop; R. H. Codrington's *The Melanesians* [1891] was a work that set a style for this kind of study.[5] Anthropologists like the Oxford don, Sir Edward Burnett Tylor, revealed that many codes whose moral specifications were opposed to each other had, at certain times and in specific places, been means of human survival.)

A variety of codes made one less willing to suppose that all the elements of a code one had happened to be born into should be given unswerving obedience. The Victorian code had been useful for one's parents, but one could also ask whether modifications of sexual mores and other matters were not in order. This question became more and more attractive in the early decades of the twentieth century when, to knowledge of the great deviations among the moral systems by which men lived, was added an awareness of the insights that Freud and other psychologists provided: that conventional moral prohibitions did not cancel "evil" impulses but simply drove them more deeply into a person.

Such questions empower Huxley's early inspection of the moral convictions of his elders. Huxley observed, as his novels richly indicate, another telling circumstance: his elders simply did not practice the morality they promoted. Indeed, much adult behavior manifested a basic hypocrisy. Older persons professed altruism but devoted their lives to the making of profits, whatever the cost to members of their own society. Elders acknowledged a duty to be pure in their sex lives and then indulged in secret fornication; they professed devotion to the Savior who warned against the sword, but they took up the sword which they had kept prudently sharp.

These are the hypocrisies upon which the satire of the Huxley novels batten. In the early novels it is enough to point out the failure of the pillars of society and to take malicious delight in patent discrepancies. In the later novels and essays, to the continuing and relentless mockery of this "parental" failure are added vigorous suggestions as to where the corrective to such failure lies.

A betrayal of the earlier view? No, not a betrayal, but a necessary extension of what Huxley had offered in his first work. For his satire in those early works rested on a different basis from that which supports much satire. The fierce censures of Swift and the gentler rebukes of Addison and Steele drew their strength from a confident perception of the insights which ought to guide all men of good sense and rational piety. In contrast, Huxley addressed a world in which there was no common agreement as to what ought to guide the human animal. As a young and talented writer, Huxley was free to lay his stripes on the back of Folly with an indiscriminate fury. But the pleasures of such castigation are exhaustible. Huxley, in the 1930's, sought to understand his disgust and fury.

II *The Foreground: the Mind*

Thus, any sketch of the mind of Aldous Huxley must include a fairly extensive analysis of the positive convictions which animated his work from the early 1930's onward. But he had no system; in fact, he is tireless in his expression of warnings against fixed systems of thought:

It is fear of the labyrinthine flux and complexity of phenomena that has driven men to philosophy, to science, to theology—fear of the complex reality driving them to invent a simpler, more manageable, and, there-fore, consoling fiction. . . . Weary with much wandering in the maze of phenomena, frightened by the inhospitable strangeness of the world, men have rushed into the systems prepared for them by philosophers and founders of religions. . . .[6]

As this passage suggests, Huxley, when he inveighs against sys-tem, has in mind some scheme like that of Calvin, or a rationalist philosophy like that of Descartes, who has fixed on some one fact about man (man, the thinking animal). Such schemes have in common a selection of certain facts about man and a willed blind-ness to other cogent facts. Thinkers have no right to make a selec-tion of facts about man. Careful inspection is likely to show that man has other drives which lie outside a particular systematizing of human life. For example, man has the obligation to turn away from morbid contemplation of a "holy face" in a church; he must enter the public square where the duties of barter and of joy also await him.[7]

As Huxley sees the problem, an adequate interpretation of hu-man life must not stem from an abstraction that impoverishes the rich complexity of human experience. Instead, a proper interpre-tation of human life enables man to respond to a very wide range of possibilities. Such an interpretation points to altered and better lines of action simply because it has been made; it does not need the support of church councils and papal pronouncements. It does not require the relentless logic of philosophers, who move from simplified accounts of man's nature to conclusions that do violence to man's nature.

Yet, despite these warnings against system, there is a basic con-sistency, even to the point of tedious repetition, in Huxley's later descriptions of man. Certain settled conclusions lead Huxley to speak, obsessively, of the chances for human success. The possibil-ity of human success lies in the recognition that man is an "am-phibious animal"—"Floundering between time and eternity, we are amphibians and must accept the fact." [8] Systems, in Huxley's pejorative sense, rest on the assumption that man is really only one kind of animal. Is man really just a creature compact of the dark blood of which Lawrence spoke—or is his essence that of a being called to be the child of God, at the cost of denial of sex and blood or even of the chance to pursue the pleasure and profit in the marketplace? With a characteristic biological analogy.[9] Huxley asserts that man's destiny must be realized—as is that of the frog at various points of its life-cycle—in water and on solid earth. One must add that, for Huxley, man's destiny must also be realized in "air," if "air" may serve here to represent the life of the spirit.

But, unlike the cyclic frog, man is three beings at once. He is an animal with some of his instinctual inheritance intact. He is a conscious, reasoning, social creature living in terms of the moral code of his society, with what prudence and intelligence he can summon to aid him in this portion of his existence. And man can be a creature of "air" or spirit who is responsive to the "ground" or divine principle that supports or informs all existence, human or otherwise.

Despite this multiplicity, man is for Huxley a single being. True, man has the power to live only as an animal, or man has the capacity to realize his destiny entirely within the framework of current social custom. But, if he chooses, man has the chance to go beyond sense and instinct (animal) and ordinary good and evil (social and rational), and to become a child not so much of personal deity as of the "Clear Light" [10] where he merges with Nirvana, the ground of all being.[11]

For it is Huxley's not particularly novel thesis that man can perceive, behind or above all that sense and society present him, the principle, the ground of being, that has allowed to come into existence what we hastily call "basic reality." Huxley has learned, from mystics both Western and Eastern, that "basic reality" is more inclusive than the wisdom of either instinct or society. This reality is best not called God, for that word brings with it a train of Christian associations that have turned men aside from the All. For the ground of being is not a person to whom one may offer the love and obedience proper to a kind parent or just leader. "Enlightenment" and "deliverance" come only "when God is thought of as the Perennial Philosophy affirms Him to be—immanent as well as transcendent, supra-personal as well as personal—

and when religious practices are adapted to this conception." [12]
God or the ground of being is something more than a force—as
Christians are wont to say—who orders historical experience and
yet is above that experience or waiting at its terminus; the All is
the matrix from which all experience comes and to which, if one
wills, all experience can return.

Thus, in Huxley's opinion, it is better to subtract from all our
assertions about the life of the senses and from any social gesture
any excessive confidence that there is a firm link between these
portions of our existence and the ground of all existence. There is
doubtless a correspondence, but it is a shifting one, likely to dismay persons who would like to discover absolutes on the instinctual and conscious levels of their existence. It is better to follow
the greatest mystics and say of these two levels, "Nothing, nothing," as did St. John of the Cross, or "Neti, neti" ("not this, not
this") as did the Buddha. That which supports and informs instinct and consciousness is not an entity to which readily intelli-
gible terms can be applied.

But to ask if this ground exists or does not exist is an improper
question since "existence" is a term that man's particular experience of duration has generated in him. To ponder if the ground,
the "Clear Light" (a key-phrase in *Island*[13]), is good or evil and
if it rewards virtue and punishes vice is also improper.

It is interesting to note—and this is a way of pointing up a
summary of Huxley's view of man—that he is in effect offering his
readers translations or transformations of two key Christian
terms: the "fall" and "grace"; and to see what the transformation
comes to is a useful preparation for specific inspection of a good
many of Huxley's works. In his view of man's situation and what
can alleviate it, Huxley often implies that the "fall" was not the
offense of the first man, Adam, who made improper use of God-
given freedom when he followed his own will rather than God's
will *for* him. In the Huxleyan universe, the "fall" was rather an
offense or, at the very least, an incapacity on the part of the
ground of being itself. The ground, in some way that cannot be
understood, allowed what man calls the world and consequently
the life of instinct and the life of society to come into existence
and, in Shelley's phrase, stain "the white radiance of Eternity." In
the divine ground, so far as man can judge, there is neither time
nor place, but only light or nothingness devoid of anything like

personality or event. From this strange nothingness emerged the physical world, man's sense of his separate self (personality), and the interplay of separate selves that makes up history. This emergence constitutes a kind of "fall," a decline from absolute being to what is called common-sense reality.

This impression about the true nature of the "fall"—it took place before the Garden of Eden rather than in that garden—is the one that Huxley encourages us to form. In consequence, even at its best, ordinary human life can amount to only a kind of achieved imperfection. This imperfection is overcome by rare persons who manage, in mystical experience, a temporary cancellation of the rest of their "amphibious" nature.

The "fall" of the "Clear Light" into fractured and imperfect variety (the created world) may remind one, among other things, of the Gnosticism of the early Christian centuries; similar assertions about creation were made by that underground religious faith. When Gnostics spoke of the dissipation of the primal Monad into inferior monads and their actions of creation, they unwittingly anticipated Huxley's estimate of created existence. Huxley's unsympathetic remarks about the Old Testament and its warlike, vindictive God are modern versions of the Gnostic conviction that creation itself was an act foreign to the perfection of the unitary divine principle.[14]

Huxley also offers a modern version of the task that faced the Gnostic who wished to work out for himself the countermovement of the divine "fall" into the act of creation. As with the Gnostics, so it is sometimes with Huxley: an important human task is that of rising from the condition in which, through no fault of his own, man finds himself. As to how a man is to put behind himself the variety that his sense of his separate personality and the thrust of his particular desires keep before him, it is well to note, first, that the Huxleyan model man will succeed in his high task only intermittently. Unlike the Gnostics and their counterparts in the ancient East, Huxley does not think that there is a possibility of a permanent cancellation of the inferior levels of man's nature. Ancient wisdom indeed aids us to reach the third level of "air" and "clear light." For Huxley, similar wisdom does not allow man to cut himself off permanently from the life of instinct and of intelligence and social impression. As in *Island*, the person who succeeds at this task of union with the ground of being will not enjoy that admirable state very long. Rather, it is man's destiny, as the mixed creature he is, to "return" to the embraces of sex or, less sensationally, to the struggles of a "good" society against the evils of democratic nationalism or a still more evil fascism.

This insistence on "return" records Huxley's faithfulness to his view of complexity in man. The pleasures of vision must inevitably give way to renewed labors for the enlightenment of men who exist beset by desire and limited by the moral convictions of their own time.

When man rises, he does so with the aid of a kind of "grace." This "grace" is, like the "fall" just discussed, in contrast with the Christian one. The Christian achieves his vision not by means of acts which he initiates; rather, he shares the merit which God, in the person of Christ and in Christ's death, made available to men. Such a view of the power ("grace") which allows certain men to achieve completeness would be inacceptable to Huxley. For him, deity as unity or pervasive nullity is continuingly present in the material and social world which the "fall" into diversity created.

The benefits issuing from such a deity are available not because of an event at one point in time (the death on the cross); they are present anywhere and everywhere once a man has seen through the illusions that ordinarily pass for reality. Illumination and rectification of the error do not come to man because of a personal and individual relation to a divine being and his sacrificed son. The "Clear Light" has none of the marks that qualify a person; indeed, it is the proper aim of each man to cease, at exalted moments, to be a person himself. He must instead teach himself to respond to the basic unity which diversity ("desire," say the Buddhists) distracts him from. From this point of view, "grace"—the power to respond to the divine unity and to merge with it—is always in each man's possession, if he but knew it.[15]

The later Huxley's wish is to make each man aware of the continuing presence of this sort of grace or aid. Once aware that what he desires he already possesses, each man can execute the last step of what might be called a triple movement. The process of canceling all impressions of diversity is but a third and concluding step, a termination of the struggle that commenced when "Clear Light" was refracted into the many colors that make up existence for the ordinary man. Man is involved in a life of instinct which he shares with the animals, a life that is spontaneous and unreflective. Man,

by developing powers of reason, moves onward from this condition (but paradoxically, in Huxley, does not leave this condition
behind). He moves forward to perceptions of good and evil that
are at once a progress upward and yet a kind of minor "fall" of his
own. He abandons the obvious beneficence of purely instinctual
life (here is a kind of salute of the older Huxley to the element of
truth in the theories of D. H. Lawrence) and moves toward language, the basis for all the achievements that one considers to be
specifically human.[16] Allied to this movement toward language
are the achievements that engage Huxley's attention in many of
his essays: painting, sculpture, music, architecture, and literature.
They are, one might say, of deep interest to him when he is meditating on man's rational capacities. They are uninstructive to him
when he presses beyond those capacities; art is the child of time
and cannot claim the parentage of eternity.[17]

This movement from the instinctual to consciousness that is
both analytical and creative puts man at odds with his biological
inheritance. Man's sexual impulse—to take an example crucial
with Huxley—is not any longer the impulse which, with proper
periodicity, leads animals to rut. Instead, man struggles to make
rational comment on his sexuality, adorns it with the fabrications
of art, and is even tempted to eschew it in the name of "higher"
human activities; and this struggle can be read as depressing evidence that man's instinctual ties have been weakened and disordered. With the supervening life of the mind, the sexual urge is
associated with romantic love (an "elevating" action) and yet, at
the same time, is involved in clouds of guilt. Thus man, at this
intermediate stage of the triple movement, is neither angel nor
beast, as in Pascal's phrase; it would be simpler for man to be one
or the other.

Yet man cannot return to the instinctual, "triggered" patterns of
animal sexual action. Rampant sexuality among *human* beings is,
for Huxley, not a regaining of the simple and lost animal inno-
cence; it is a perversion of human sexuality. Indeed, any return to
the conditions of animal rut and battle is a perversion of the benefits which the rule of intelligence has opened up to the human
animal.

Man must, therefore, be content, in large portions of his existence, to respond to the pointers offered by reason and not go back
to a level below that which knowledge of good and evil, of beauty

and ugliness, provides. This insight, however, must not render man complacent on this second level—content with where he is. Instead, man must go beyond what he possesses as a being who has gained the profits of the discourse of sweet reason. He must try to move toward the last stage of the triple movement—toward what that discourse points to but cannot by itself construct. Beyond philosophy, the work of reason, and beyond esthetic harmonies, the work of a kind of practical reason, lies the "Perennial Philosophy," which is not philosophy in the usual sense but the result of the illumination or "grace" that is immanent in each man. This illumination is a "not-ourselves"—at least, it is foreign to man's instinctual and rational self.

In summary, the "fall" of unity into diversity, the secondary "fall" of the separate human being into rationality,[10] is corrected only when man goes beyond the common sense and reason which keep him at his supposedly important task of being a discriminating person. Only then does he merge with that sea of being from which he and all that exists have emerged. This last step—which no animal needs to take since he lacks the capacity for it—is the step which the Buddha advised. Men are not really separate from the objects which they are able to contemplate with their discriminating, divisive rationality. For beyond the rational "I am not that" is the mystical "Thou art that." [19] All mystics have known, Huxley is sure, that man is one, or can be one, with the objects which he contemplates. In the famous Eastern figure, the drop of water that is man's individual consciousness falls into the pool that is the universal and unitary consciousness; in that pool man blessedly loses his sense of apartness and distinction.

Such an experience, in contrast with the unnecessarily complex Christian account, involves no transaction between one person (divine and all-powerful) and another (weak and human). The last phrase of the triple movement is not a relationship between man and some transcendent deity. It is only a human exploitation of knowledge that man in the first place may acquire from mystics and teachers like Aldous Huxley, but that, as later experience shows, man has always had.[20]

This full human journey does not, in Huxley's opinion, amount to an impoverishment of man's participation in either instinctual or rational activity. Illumination and vision do not terminate his sensuality; instead, they give sensuality an enlightening context to which animals cannot aspire and of which most human beings do not dream. Illumination and vision also refine the workings of rationality and of all else that is creative in man; they endow these non-instinctive powers with a sense of their proper limits.

In this outline of Huxley's thought, there is the body of conviction that gradually took shape after Huxley had terminated his time of laying waste, his period of no-saying. In his novels and casual essays, in his lengthy and repetitive tracts for his confused time,[21] Huxley gives what he regards as instructive answers to the problems of a devastated, empty world. The answers may or may not have intrinsic value: this, each reader must decide for himself. What is more certain is the usefulness of an account like this one for indicating the element of order and direction in Huxley's work. Beneath the variety of form and subject-matter is, finally, a simplicity of hope. The hope is doubtless a result of strength and limitation in Huxley's own temperament; it is also, to a considerable extent, a definition of that temperament.

CHAPTER 3

Fiction: Crome Yellow *to* Point Counter Point

DURING the years from the appearance of *Crome Yellow* (1921) to *Point Counter Point* (1928) and several collections of stories,[1] Huxley was also writing essays on assorted and often recondite topics;[2] he produced a travel journal, *Jesting Pilate* (1926); and he offered to his public in *Proper Studies* (1927) a rehearsal of his current beliefs. Also, in this period, as well as earlier, appeared collections of his poetry[3]—poetry remarkably like the verses produced by various personages in his novels.[4]

This listing of the work done during the 1920's is but a forecast of the unremitting literary labor of Huxley's life, his career; in them we see a man facing and trying to solve some of the challenges to man that lie in the twentieth-century situation. Huxley's early fiction is an attack, sometimes frontal, sometimes lateral, on the questions that the twentieth-century situation addresses to man. Much of the early fiction is a performance that argues, with satiric distortion and also with explicit statement, that the solutions offered by previous generations are either inadequate or outright incorrect. Such a judgment—to the delight of many early readers—produced a work of demolition; it is a labor that can be observed in both the novels and the short stories.[5]

If this characterization of Huxley's early work as a novelist is just, then Huxley is at odds with the assumptions and literary practice of many of his contemporaries. Huxley, like his great friend, D. H. Lawrence, did not hesitate to burden chosen characters with discourses that were plainly the author's direct address to his readers. Huxley's later novels are clearly propaganda for his enlightening opinions. In large part, if not entirely, this early work is a preparation (often unconscious) for the later propaganda.

That the writer of fiction may or should be concerned with the projection of explicit social and ethical insights is a practice that puts Huxley to one side of the mainstream of British and Ameri-

can fiction in the twentieth century. The conviction obviously detaches Huxley from what one might call the simple-minded realism of Arnold Bennett, whose excuse for much in his fiction is that
the object—provincial English life, the great hotel—is there. Huxley's estimate of what may be done with prose fiction is, however,
opposed to more than the Bennetts of his world.[6] It is significant
that Huxley, omnivorous reader that he was and thorough reporter of what he had been reading, has very little to say of the
art of prose fiction as practiced by many of his distinguished contemporaries. It is true that he rejects the meticulous and plodding
realism of Arnold Bennett and asserts—if the lady novelist of
Huxley's *Those Barren Leaves* and Miss Penny of the story, "Nuns
at Luncheon," can be taken as speaking for him—that a narrative
should be free to soar beyond the tedious presentation of what is
simply there.

Miss Thriplow of the novel remarks of her public—and Huxley
seems to have in mind his own early following—"They like my
books because they're smart and unexpected and rather paradoxi-
cal and cynical and elegantly brutal. They don't see how serious it
all is. They don't see the tragedy and the tenderness underneath."
She then states what, in her own opinion, her fiction really is; and
her formula is an apt statement of the effect of much of Huxley's
own fiction: ". . . I'm trying to do something new—a chemical
compound of all the categories. Lightness and tragedy and loveli-
ness and wit and fantasy and realism and irony and sentiment all
combined." [7]

In his pursuit of this goal, Huxley pays little attention to great
ranges of British life; those who do manual labor fail to draw his
attention.[8] His mind is chiefly caught by the behavior of the
upper-middle-class, preferably those who are intellectually complex. For the London poor, for the lower-class Italians who people
the middle distances of a good many stories,[9] Huxley has the attention that a scientist has for strange and unforeseen forms of
animal life; these forms can be described, but it is too much to
expect that they can be entered into.

The fact is that, when Huxley follows his belief that the novelist
must be free to cut and patch reality as his own satiric rejection of
nonsense suggests, he is at odds not only with the somewhat mechanical tenets of Arnold Bennett's Zola-inspired realism but also
with the artistic practices of great contemporaries. Much British

and American fiction of Huxley's time expressed the view that true realism, true reproductions of the texture of life, had to go far beyond a mechanical report of surface fact: dress, conversation, and physical gesture. The delicate acts of selection to be seen in Katherine Mansfield and Virginia Woolf; the significance that Henry James had earlier attributed to posture and phrase; the brooding penetration that Joseph Conrad brought to bear on a chance human outcry—these were all efforts to go beneath the miscellaneous surface of a world that Arnold Bennett and H. G. Wells, in a novel like *The History of Mr. Polly* (1910), had been content to record.

Beneath the surface that fired the imaginations of Bennett and Wells—those two "uncles" of British fiction, in Rebecca West's phrase[10]—were crucially important springs of human action and sensibility. The detection of these springs challenged many writers to be imitators of human life at its center, where will and memory, intelligence and instinct, have their complex interplay. Such study may indeed suggest ideas about what man is and what he may become. But those concepts are products of writers' efforts to be faithful to man as he is: acting, thinking, hoping. Although one can speak of the ideas of Henry James, Joseph Conrad, and Virginia Woolf, such ideas are the end-product of faithfulness to specific persons suffering and willing.

Huxley's practice puts him as much at odds with this latter approach to reality as he is with a meticulous and uninspired realism. Huxley's fiction takes its rise from specific ideas that he has about man; for ideas *about* human beings rather than human beings are Huxley's points of departure. Joseph Conrad's presentation of a succession of human destinies may indeed add up to some general statements about human dignity and hope; but the destinies he chooses to present are not obviously manipulated materials (as in Huxley, or in much of D. H. Lawrence) that illustrate dogmatic convictions antecedent to the novelist's inspection of some invented destiny.

To say that ideas *about* human experience take precedence over an attentive and reverent cherishing of it in Huxley's novels is a definition rather than a necessarily adverse judgment of his approach to writing fiction. At any rate, the perception allows one to account for the absence of certain complex effects of design and texture that readers of much modern fiction expect. Huxley's fiction does not give intense pleasure of this sort, for what is firm in much of Huxley's fiction is the continuous polemic drive and the subordination to it of event and the delineation of persons.

Three great contemporaries—Joyce, Proust, and Gide—win some sort of attention from Huxley.[11] There is a rather obvious imitation of Joyce's night-town, coffee-stall scene in Huxley's *Antic Hay;*[12] perhaps one can see in the experiment with time in the fairly late *Eyeless in Gaza* (1936) a slight reflection of Joyce's —and Proust's—attention to time as a medium essential to human experience. And, in Huxley's *Those Barren Leaves* (1925), there is an occasional Proust-like emphasis on the relation of the present and the past.[13] But a theme which is the essence of Proust's work is, with Huxley, a mechanical device which serves to open up one more attack on Huxley's central problem: the representation in fiction of fixed tastes and ideas of the writer's own that reality can be drawn on to illustrate but not to establish. In short, Huxley is not an artistic innovator; he merely uses some other writer's device if it serves his purpose. It is significant that Huxley's novels and tales have not tempted academic critics to feats of explication as have the ambiguities in Katherine Mansfield's "The Garden Party," Joyce's "Araby," and Conrad's "The Heart of Darkness."

If there is any device that is properly Huxley's own or that he makes his own, it is the one that may be called "counterpoint." The device is used very consciously in *Point Counter Point*, but it is frequent in all his fiction. In one version, this device effects a sudden switch from one scene to another;[14] the arresting change of scene and persons amounts to an inharmonious contrast between one set of human pretensions and another. A modified form of the device exists within a scene when the words a person speaks are played off against the thoughts that are passing through his mind.[15] Similarly the speech of one person in a scene is put in sharp and irrelevant contrast to the chatter of another person.[16]

Indeed, any inspection of Huxley's fiction leads to the conclusion that his chief guide to the manipulation of event is the writer's desire to establish ironical cross-reference. Such cross-reference—in an early novel like *Antic Hay* (1923)—is for the sake of irony itself; the only meaning life has lies in its basic inconsequence. Later, the same device is used more systematically to point to the "amphibious" nature of man and even to man's need to transcend the effects of irony and inconsequence that are all most men know of life. The effect of such cross-reference is often brilliant and telling;[17] but sometimes, one must grant, it is merely mechanical. Ironical cross-reference seems to be only a means of getting on with the tale and underlining once more ideas and impressions that are already familiar to the reader of Huxley.

I   Crome Yellow

Chiefly from the four novels of the 1920's—along with the shorter narrative works—comes the popular image of Aldous Huxley as a knight who tilted against the forces of prudery, obscurantism, and hypocrisy. If these early novels—*Crome Yellow, Antic Hay, Those Barren Leaves,* and *Point Counter Point*—and short stories now seem less emanicipating than they actually were, one has to recall that younger men have spaded more deeply in the fields that Huxley helped open to cultivation: parents are selfish and batten on their young; conventional upper-class educations represents a conspiracy to keep the young in the dark as long as possible; religion is a set of chains useful to the hypocritical defenders of the status quo; and, above all, love is not an ideal and pure emotion but a composite of sensuality and selfishness that ends (or so for Huxley) in an even deeper solitude than that which preceded embrace. Today, in the second half of the twentieth century, these insights are commonplace.

Indeed, a prolonged and intensive reading of the novels of Huxley can produce impatience with a writer who, early and late, announced these truths as if they were constantly fresh news about the human lot. These concepts were indeed once—it must be insisted—fresh news, brought to readers not only by Huxley but, in slightly varying ways, by Ronald Firbank, Carl Van Vechten, Evelyn Waugh (somewhat later), and numerous other writers. But Huxley, from *Crome Yellow* onward, was chief among those who introduced a generation to the bitter necessity of disillusionment: a state of mind which, as the success of Huxley's novels indicated, was much to their liking.

Among the four novels of the 1920's—certainly in comparison with most of the short stories of the same time[18]—*Crome Yellow* is easily the best on esthetic grounds. It is perhaps the best, on these grounds, that Huxley ever wrote; but it is not the most interesting and the most significant since there are other novels in which Huxley says more about his convictions and his era. Except

for a few passages in *Crome Yellow* in which the fledgling poet
Denis Stone speculates on the pains of man the solitary being—
lapses which forecast later earnestness—the young Huxley in
Crome Yellow blends the novels of Thomas Love Peacock of a
century earlier with those of George Meredith. In Peacock's novels, English eccentrics gather at country houses to ride their hob-
bies across the lawns; in the novels of Meredith, a large company
of characters talk with something like the wit of the long-lapsed
Restoration drama. But, though the brilliant, unsparing light of
Crome Yellow may have been suggested to Huxley by earlier
writers, his expression of youthful confidence and competence
falls over the terraces and gardens of *Crome Yellow* and bathes
the parlors with a brilliance that shines without remission.

The design of the novel is quite simple. A young poet, Denis
Stone, comes down to Crome, the estate of Henry Wimbush, for a
house-party. (In *Crome Yellow* the country house continues to
serve the fictitious purposes it had been put to by many earlier
writers, from Jane Austen and Disraeli to Henry James: a kind of
substitute for the royal palace of older drama and fairy tale.) The
party is, for Huxley, a transparent excuse for assembling a company of eccentrics, some witty and some boring. Among the witty
is discursive Mr. Scogin, reptilian in appearance and the very
archetype of all the worldly wise, erudite persons who stroll in
and out of other Huxley novels; one of his counterparts is Mr. Cardan of *Those Barren Leaves*. Scogin, who is able to drop cross-
references that would send most people to an encyclopedia, is responsive to art and indifferent to the claims on him of human
beings, educated and uneducated. Also quite clever is the host,
Henry Wimbush, who is writing a history of the house he owns.
He reads to his guests sections of this history, and one of these is a
heartless and perfect tale of an ancestral dwarf, "Sir Hercules." [19]
For Wimbush, the past is more real than the present; ancient
wooden drains are more fascinating than the artifacts of his own
time.

A little less witty but highly talented is Gombauld, a painter,
and, Huxley adds darkly, a "Latin." Gombauld paints in a style
that crops up again in the work of another artist, Rampion of
Point Counter Point.[20] This style has gone beyond Impressionism
and Cubism in the direction of deep and symbolic meaning. (In a

very early story, "Eupompus Gave Splendor to Art by Numbers"
[1916], Huxley had already defined his own artistic taste; he tells
approvingly of the suicide of an ancient artist who became lost in
the nightmare of trying to reduce art to the condition of mathe-
matics.[21] It must be confessed that Huxley's taste in art always
comes down heavily on the side of meaning; admirers of much
modern art must find his visual esthetics as outmoded as John
Ruskin's outright moralism in *The Stones of Venice*.)

Denis, the young poet, who is capable of holding his own with
these talented persons, does not have to worry about most of the
other persons. His hostess, Mrs. Wimbush, plays the horses with
the aid of horoscopes and is also enamored of the treacly discourses about the infinite by the writings of Mr. Barbecue-Smith.
This "nonsense" has some rather embarrassing points of contact
with Huxley's later positive views about self-discipline and self-
transcendence in *Time Must Have a Stop* (1944) and in *The
Perennial Philosophy* (1945). But only mockery of pretentious
nonsense is intended in *Crome Yellow* when Denis confesses to
Barbecue-Smith that he has not read *Pipe-Lines to the Infinite*.
Barbecue-Smith explains: "It's just a little book about the connection of the Subconscious with the Infinite. Get into touch with the
Subconscious and you are in touch with the Universe." Barbecue-
Smith adds that his task is to canalize the Infinite: "I bring it
down through the pipes to work the turbines of my conscious
mind." The reader is in sympathy with Denis's rejoinder: "Like
Niagara." [22] Similarly, the reader participates in the implied superiority of Denis to the dreary religious speculation of Mr. Bodiham, whose attacks on "higher criticism" only discredit a whole
range of rear-guard theological thinking.[23]

There are also young women trooping across the scene: Anne, a
Wimbush niece, who displays a slight degree of interest in both
Denis and Gombauld, and Mary Bracegirdle (is her name—a rare
thing in Huxley's mind—symbolic in intent?), who has had the
misfortune to discover Freud's teachings but who simplifies Freudian doctrine: "It's always dangerous to repress one's instincts.
I'm beginning to detect in myself symptoms like the ones you read
of in the books." [24] But, when Mary sleeps with another visitor (a
poet and a Catholic), she is hurt by his sudden departure. Finally,
there is Jenny Mullion, whose deafness causes comments that are

at comic cross-purpose with the remarks of others and who avenges herself by drawing unflattering caricatures of her fellow guests.

This listing, in large part, predicts the dramatis personae of later novels. There are the very intelligent and instructed, like Scogin and Denis; one of their functions, for Huxley and for the reader, is to look down on other persons and to judge them. Characters like Mary Bracegirdle, who have taken a short cut with the aid of Freud or someone else, *think* that they are intelligent and instructed; and others, like Barbecue-Smith and the Reverend Bodiham, deserve only heartless laughter. Later novels add to such a range of characters people who are simply "good" (Mrs. Chelifer in *Those Barren Leaves* and Mrs. Quarles in *Point Counter Point*) with a goodness that an intelligent and instructed person can name and even admire, though it would not occur to him to imitate such virtue. Also absent from the cast of characters in *Crome Yellow* is the person capable of mindless violence, one who, like Spandrell in *Point Counter Point,* has cut himself adrift from all values, intellectual or moral.

Plot, in *Crome Yellow,* moves the characters in and out of drawing rooms and, in some instances, of different pairs of arms. Plot does not—and here lies a difference between *Crome Yellow* and other novels—contain events whose galvanic charge stirs persons into violent action, deep ranges of introspection, and unalterable decisions or their simulacra. There is just enough event in *Crome Yellow* to keep the characters talking and no more, and these events are simple. Anne Wimbush sprains an ankle and avoids sexual entanglements. Mary sleeps in a rooftop pavilion (once the location of an ancient privy—a human convenience that has great power over Huxley's imagination) and receives visits from Ivor Lombard, the Catholic poet. A fair is held on the lawn; Scogin disguises himself as a female gypsy and tells fortunes that draw on his insight into the minds of the stupid and simple. Finally—for the novel has to end—Denis Stone sends himself a telegram and leaves forever Crome and its delights.

These incidents are presented with a cynical, light style that gives the reader a sense that he and the author are looking down on everyone except, perhaps, Mr. Scogin when he is launched on some serious discourse on religion or birth regulation (a topic that anticipates *Brave New World* a decade later). There is not, one should note, much interchange between characters. There are a few conversations, such as those between Denis and Anne, in which talk is real communication. Otherwise, what commences as a scene with two or more persons conversing ends in a monologue that may air the interesting concepts of a man like Scogin or may give fools like Barbecue-Smith or the Reverend Mr. Bodiham the rope they need to hang themselves. Denis, the person in this novel who laments man's tendency to fall into monologue, reflects after a frustrating interchange with the deaf Jenny: "Parallel straight lines . . . meet only at infinity. He might talk forever of care-charmer sleep and she of meteorology till the end of time. Did one ever establish contact with anyone? We are all parallel straight lines. Jenny was only a little more parallel than most." [25] The other intelligent persons in *Crome Yellow*, unlike many such characters in later novels, discover no reason to lament their solitude; the stupid, of course, are incapable of such discovery. And the "good" stand in no need of it.

II   Antic Hay

Huxley's second novel, *Antic Hay* (1923), is one in which the artistically disturbing division between the satiric vision realized in *Crome Yellow* and explicit didactic exhortation makes its first appearance. One might even expect, in terms of forecast, this second element eventually to take over. The fact is that Huxley, even in his most serious and instructive novels, is not able to forgo satirizing views that are, to his mind, manifestly wrong and stupid. Contempt, the mark of his satire, if not of all satire, continues in *Antic Hay*. But it must share the scene with Huxley's effort to go beyond satire—to plunge into the depths of uncertainty and human nullity where satire cannot operate. Satire, one may note, is written out of confidence. The kind of reserved sympathy that Huxley is able to summon at times comes from an uncertainty as to what man is and what man can do.

Huxley's reserved sympathy, in the later novels, is animated by solutions that resolve this uncertainty and that offer confused men something better than what intellectual arrogance (like Scogin's in *Crome Yellow*, like Mercaptan's in *Antic Hay*) can suggest. Huxley's attitude toward root-stupidity undergoes no growth; the

horoscope-betting Mrs. Wimbush and Barbecue-Smith, the offerer
of the instant infinite, are but the vanguard of a contemptible
company.

Satire is certainly still the dominant note of *Antic Hay*. Only in
isolated sections of the novel—as in the nightmare ride which the
world-weary Myra Viveash and her companion, Theodore Gumbril Junior, take through London[26]—appears a presentation of
human reaction that is marked by non-satiric sympathy, if not by
the hope for the correction and improvement of human behavior
that later characterizes Huxley. In many portions of *Antic Hay*
Huxley remains the confident satirist that he was in *Crome
Yellow;* and as such a writer he operates in many of his short
stories of this period.[27]

The center of *Antic Hay* rests on the experience of Theodore
Gumbril, Junior, but he is abandoned from time to time for other
tempting quarry. Theodore, a young man nauseated by the facile
piety and the hollow curriculum of the school where he teaches,
gives up his job to return to his father's house, to the literary and
artistic London—which is not much better than the academic
world. Theodore finds hopes, ambitions, and self-delusions among
the persons he meets. Even in the parental hall, he can observe his
father working on an architectural model for a better and nobler
London[28]—a model that enshrines the hopes of the agnostic father and that draws from Huxley the sort of scorn that he offered
all utopian futures in *Brave New World*. Theodore can also observe the emptiness of the pursuit of Classical learning on the part
of his father's friend Porteus—whose son, alas, follows too much
to the letter a certain ancient Greek perversity, homosexuality.

Outside his father's house—in the restaurants, exhibition gal-
leries, and studios of London—human delusion quite as laughable
exists to amuse Theodore. The young man finds amusement in the
efforts of Casimir Lypiatt, an older artist, to go beyond Cubism
and abstraction to a sort of painting that will recover man's power
to convey a meaning that has been ebbing from the avant-garde
painting of the time—significant meaning rather than the "significant form" which Huxley's contemporary, critic Roger Fry, was
defending. Lypiatt is, of course, destined to fail. Theodore can
turn in other directions and still smile. He can feel aloof from the
scientific study of the kidney that is the *raison d'être* of a physiologist named Shearwater; it is Shearwater who, in the last scene of

the novel, is wildly peddling a bicycle in a sealed room to test the quantity of perspiration involved. Theodore can find in Mercaptan the emptiness of a purely esthetic criticism based on eighteenth century sensibilities.

Finally, he can also study Coleman the diabolist—a first and effective sketch of the character of Spandrell in *Point Counter Point.* Coleman and the later Spandrell are English versions of Dostoyevsky's Stavrogin in *The Possessed:* a man who has put all moral norms behind him and has said, "Evil, be thou my good." Coleman, young Theodore can observe, delights in twisting the phrases of Christian piety to make them express his own odd sensibility; he lives with a mistress whom he loathes and who loathes him, and he takes delight in increasing the moral confusion of other persons (one of his victims is the son of the Classical grammarian; another, the wife of Shearwater, the physiologist).

Besides these chief characters who make up Gumbril's London world, there is the Socialist tailor, Bojanus, who works with Theodore on the perfection of Theodore's great invention, Gumbril's Patented Small Clothes. Theodore's hard hours in the school chapel have suggested to him that trousers with pneumatic seats would be a boon to mankind. To popularize his product, Theodore turns to the ruthless entrepreneur, Boldero, wise and cynical beyond his era in his knowledge of how to manipulate the fears and inferiorities of mankind and to increase the sale of the Small Clothes.

One of the most brilliant chapters in the novel recounts Boldero's plans for his insidious campaign. Boldero explains how important it is to play on the snobbism of the consumer: "to exploit that painful sense of inferiority which the ignorant and ingenuous always feel in the presence of the knowing." He adds: "We've got to make our trousers the Thing—socially right as well as merely personally comfortable. We've got to imply somehow that it's bad form not to wear them." [29] Boldero's discourse to Theodore is, in fact, a handbook of advertising strategy that is still not superseded. Readers pleased with the energy and knowingness that Huxley summons in this and other passages of *Antic Hay* doubtless regret that he heard, in later years, the siren call of non-satiric tasks that are already a minor note in this novel.

In the depiction of two of the three main female characters of *Antic Hay,* this call is responded to. Rose Shearwater, the affected and seducible wife of the physiologist, is still drawn chiefly with satiric strokes; a compound of sensuality and cultural snobbery, she neither stirs nor deserves sympathy. Neglected by her husband and eager for "better things," she is a willing victim to Gumbril's fantastic seduction; for Theodore dons a false beard so that he can command the sexual mana that, he judges, inheres in the real whiskers of Coleman the diabolist. Later, Rose submits easily to the somewhat different wiles of Mercaptan and his eighteenth-century sofa.

In contrast to this heartless presentation of Rose, the bored, fretful Myra Viveash is drawn with much serious attention to the shallowness of her existence. Here is an attention that leaves satire behind, for Huxley is plainly disturbed and not just amused by the disorientation of this privileged child of the twentieth century. Myra's dalliance with Lypiatt, Shearwater, and even Theodore is not merely laughable; it expresses her fear of the passage of time. At one point, Myra cries out: "Only time kills." [30] This fear reaches its culmination in a long taxi-ride that Myra and Theodore take through nighttime London. This ride that traces and retraces the streets of the city, is, thanks to Myra's discontented and insatiable spirit, a Walpurgisnacht in which the fires are not those of hell but the night traceries of the electrical displays of Piccadilly Circus. Myra fears that she will be overwhelmed by nothingness, by a lack of essential meaning in her life. At the outset of the ride, she sighs: "We're all in the vacuum"; [31] and nothing occurs in the course of the evening to prove her wrong. Hers is a fear that Huxley cannot laugh at—as he can at the fears of the lower classes that Boldero proposes to exploit on behalf of Gumbril's Patented Small Clothes.

Also beyond the limits of satire is the presentation of Gumbril's second mistress, Emily, a "good" young woman. Emily, Gumbril soon learns, was repulsed by the sexual manners of the elderly and "fatherly" man she had married. But she responds to Gumbril's gentle approaches, and soon he discards his beard in her presence. But at a crucial point in their relationship, Gumbril fails to go to the country to be with Emily; tempted by Myra, he submits the tender relation to a lethal mockery that he knows is a betrayal. "He thought of Emily in her native quiet among the flowers; in a cottage altogether too cottagey, with honeysuckles and red ramblers and hollyhocks—though, on second thoughts, none of them would be blooming yet, would they?—happily, in white muslin, extracting from the cottage piano the easier sections of the Arietta." [32] When he finally tries to keep his rural tryst, Emily has fled; she has estimated justly the shallowness of her lover. Huxley clearly regards Theodore's failure as less than laughable.

This mystery in Gumbril—the inconclusive warfare between a corrupt will and a full knowledge of what virtue and sense advise —is not amenable to satiric representation any more than is Myra Viveash's emptiness. At this point in his record of Gumbril's adventures Huxley is faced by human complexities which a satirist would not care to handle. At such points, the sufferings of Gumbril, Emily, and Myra suggest a root-corruption in all persons and not just folly among those who are inexcusably arrogant or stupid.

Denis, the hero of *Crome Yellow*, speaks briefly of human destinies as parallel lines that do not meet.[33] This figure is developed more explicitly when Huxley investigates Myra's sensibility as she contemplates her boring involvement with Lypiatt. The point of her meditation is that the system of parallels separating people from each other gets out of order.

> Why was it that people always got involved in one's life? If only one could manage things on the principles of the railways! Parallel tracks— that was the thing. For a few miles you'd be running at the same speed. There'd be delightful conversation out of the windows. . . . And when you'd said all there was to say, you'd put on a little more steam, wave your hand, blow a kiss and away you'd go, forging ahead along the smooth, polished rails. But instead of that, there were these dreadful accidents; the points were wrongly set, the trains came crashing together. . . .[34]

Yet, Myra might have added, there are other moments when one desires this crash to take place; but too often the trains move apart, and each person is left alone with his inadequate personality, alone with the boredom that hectors Myra, alone with the guilt that pains Theodore when he fails Emily.

In the novel which follows *Antic Hay, Those Barren Leaves,* there is a section actually entitled "The Loves of the Parallels"—a phrase which underlines the point that is suggested by the relation between the corrupted Gumbril and the naïve and trusting Emily. Human beings should be capable of responding to each other's needs for comprehension and support, but—as the experience of Gumbril and many another Huxley hero suggests—they are simply not equal to the demands which other persons make on them. They run on their own tracks and only seem to meet and embrace, in love or just in friendship, another person. Huxley's repetitive and non-satiric reading of human character is, therefore, that most persons do not respond to each other as they should, as they know they should. So Emily, abandoning the lover whom her "goodness" at last allows her to read aright, is but the first of a rather large company of characters who are brutally treated by persons whose "tracks" simply take them in other directions. A similar person is Ethel Cobbett in *Point Counter Point,* who puts her head in a gas oven when she finally sees that the object of her love—Burlap the critic—has no intention of responding to her need.[35]

One may say that the tragedy that begins to stir at certain points in *Antic Hay* is one of solipsism. Such a tragedy is one in which a satirist can have little interest, for the must write from confidence in himself and his own powers, confidence that the standards of judgment which he applies are held by all well-thinking persons—persons who, one may say, travel on the very train that carries him forward. But, if a more profound analysis reveals that one, as a representative human being, is the only passenger on the train, if human contacts are generally no more than chance views of other faces pressed against train windows moving elsewhere, then the satiric verve that inspirited *Crome Yellow* must falter. Each man is alone, a solipsist; and this insight may well mark one's understanding of the clever as well as the stupid.

From such a sense of isolation comes a fierce need to speak fully to other persons, and the novels of Huxley suggests that this desire is not likely to be easily satisfied. Although some think this need to be peculiar to modern man, one may question this sweeping and flattering judgment—flattering, because it is pleasant to think that modern man has his own peculiar ailment. But one can remark that the disturbing depths of certain Huxley novels concern this kind of isolation—isolation, more often than not, of the erudite intellectual. It is only with a considerable effort—and with less effect of conviction—that Huxley presents the isolation and confusion of a simpler person, like Emily in *Antic Hay.*

This non-satiric theme is only announced in *Antic Hay,* but it commands more space in the next two novels, *Those Barren Leaves* and *Point Counter Point.* Concerning the vehicle that is human existence, Francis Chelifer observes: "With gathering momentum the trolley plunges down into vacancy"; and Huxley observes of one of his pleasure seekers in *Point Counter Point:* "The dread of solitude was chronic with her." [36] The treatment of solitude becomes still more crucial in the novels that follow the rather special interlude of *Brave New World.* These works—*Eyeless in Gaza, Time Must Have a Stop,* and others—express a belief that the tracks can indeed be brought together without the appalling crash upon which Myra Viveash meditated; they express a hope that there is some kind of term to the boredom and isolation that drive Gumbil and Myra Viveash around London in a taxi. Perhaps the embraces of "amphibious" beings may sometimes unite mind with mind and spirit with spirit instead of mere flesh with flesh.

One should note that the design of *Antic Hay* is somewhat different from that of *Crome Yellow.* In his first novel, Huxley had faith that his powers of satirical observation would sustain an almost plotless account of a country weekend. Although there are passages in *Antic Hay* that record a similar confidence—the conversations between Gumbril father and son[37] and the noisy encounter in the Soho cafe[38]—the novel really moves forward because of a series of encounters that function like the electric current that can enliven a cage of weary lions. This use of event does not have much in common with a plot which is an "action" that shapes and transforms the beings who endure it.

Huxley's characters, in general, are neither shaped nor transformed by the chain of events, as is, for example, Conrad's Lord Jim, or James's Isabel Archer in *The Portrait of a Lady.* Instead, Huxley contrives a series of shocks which—at least in the novels of the 1920's—demonstrate what the characters really are. Looking forward to his later novels, one could maintain that events there do indeed produce signal alterations. But those alterations (that of Sebastian Barnack in *Time Must Have a Stop* and that of the "goddess" in *The Genius and The Goddess*) are manifestations of discontinuity. Of Isabel Archer, one might say: her end is her beginning. Of any Huxley characters who undergo signal changes, one is forced to say the opposite. Their "ends" have little relation to their initial poses and illustrate instead Huxley's developed ideas about what human nature is capable of at its best: a merg-

ing with the All. The revolution in being is not, as with Isabel
Archer, some peculiar or individual appropriation of the buffets of
experience. With Huxley—as *Antic Hay* rather simply suggests—
the buffets serve to keep the novel going and to produce additional effects of isolation, comic or tragic.

Endlessly inventive of buffets, Huxley contrives—in *Antic Hay*
and in later novels—incidents that have great power to shock because of their unexpectedness, often by their impropriety, often
by their basic cancellation of human dignity. The parrot that interrupts the lovemaking in *Point Counter Point*,[39] the dog that
falls from the plane and spatters blood over the lovers in *Eyeless
in Gaza*,[40] Shearwater, peddling away on his bicycle in *Antic Hay*,
or Coleman stabbed by his churlish mistress[41]—most of these are
affronts to human dignity that do not instruct, and cannot be ap-
propriated by the characters who experience them as are, for example, the abandoning of the "Patna" in *Lord Jim* or Isabel's discovering of adultery in *The Portrait of a Lady*.

The shocks provided in *Antic Hay* are humiliating enough. But,
as if in prolongation of the gaiety of *Crome Yellow*, they are more
farcical and less crushing than those to be noted in *Those Barren
Leaves* or in *Point Counter Point*. Indeed, many of them seem to
be borrowed from P. G. Wodehouse. Already noted is the role of
the beard in the seduction of Rose Shearwater. Weary of her,
Gumbril sends her to an assignation with Mercaptan, the critic, to
whom Rose mentions the beard. Mercaptan, of course, judges that
Rose's earlier seducer was Coleman. One need not follow the obvious farce that spins out of such misunderstandings. They would
have their place in a somewhat scabrous Blandings Castle.

III   Those Barren Leaves

Those Barren Leaves (1925), a much longer book than the first
two, owes its length not to a grave difference in substance but
primarily to an elaboration of effects already existing in *Crome
Yellow* and *Antic Hay*. The novel is set in Italy, a country which
is, to Huxley's imagination, attractive on two counts. Italy
abounds in rich and suggestive materials for minds that wish to
meditate on the meaning of human culture as it has expressed
itself in architecture and music.[42] It is also a country whose inhabitants on the lower social levels are picturesque, unlike the
cloddish English poor around the coffee-stall in *Antic Hay*.[43] The

Italian poor are fully human—amorous and rapacious without shame for their passions. As one of the characters in the novel remarks: "In this horrible bourgeois age . . . it's only Southern people who still understand or even, I believe, feel passion"—an observation that draws agreement from another of Huxley's visitors from chilly Britain: "It is only among those whose desires and whose native idleness are fostered by the cherishing Southern heat that it [passion] has flourished and continues to flourish. . . ."[44] Because of these circumstances, the peninsula affords the English novelist an ideal setting for a book like *Those Barren Leaves,* which features a group of Anglo-Saxons who gather at the villa of a Mrs. Aldwinkle and, toward the end of the novel, take a trip to Rome and back.

Lillian Aldwinkle's villa is a country house with even more cultural reverberations than the English one in *Crome Yellow.* Thus, it is a useful setting for the discussions and love affairs. To these echoes of *Crome Yellow* is added an embellishment that is not necessarily an improvement: two fragments from the autobiography of one of the guests, Francis Chelifer. The very long first fragment gives what will come to be the usual mental history, the usual credentials, of a Huxley main character: the superior esthetic sensitivity and the disillusionment with English parents and English culture in general that intensify, if they do not create, the solipsistic effect of the "parallels" that do not meet.[45] The very short second fragment[46] seems to appear chiefly to disguise the fact that the first fragment was ill-judged since Chelifer turns out to be no more important than the other assembled guests.

Length is also added to the novel by nonfunctional descriptions that become a part of Huxley's artistic practice in most of his later work. When Francis Chelifer's autobiographical narrative is interrupted by a description of the Italian countryside, the texture of the description does not differ from that which, at another point in the novel, comes from the pen of the all-seeing author.[47] Exceptions do, however, appear: the wastes of the Maremma, carefully represented, make a useful contribution to the grotesque fate of the idiotic Miss Elver.[48] But such passages are infrequent; in general, Huxley's representations of the natural world in his novels are set pieces that decorate his narrative rather than advance it.

Generally, one can see in this long novel that many of Huxley's narrative techniques are continuations of Victorian practice, which saw a novel as made up of various fairly independent parts: dialogue, description, summarizing exposition.[49] By a kind of irony that Huxley would not savor, he is a novelist who preserves the artistic techniques of an era whose ideas he wished to discredit. As in much Victorian fiction, descriptions in Huxley's novels are not assimilated to the plight and mood of a character being put in action; indeed, the landscapes of *Those Barren Leaves* would be much the same whatever imagined attention were passing through them. In a scarcely less distracting way, the monologues of Cardan (the Scogin of this novel) are interesting essays in themselves but are irritating in a novel that sometimes has the air of moving from a beginning to an end. Cardan on clothes as an indicator of social custom or on the usefulness of dead languages is quite entertaining until one asks what contributions his disquisitions have made to any unfolding of action in the novel; the answer is, "None." [50]

Such difficulties are permanent limitations in the fiction of Huxley, as is his curious insensitivity to problems raised by point of view. The Chelifer fragments, which intrude a first-person narrative into one otherwise told with the freedom of the all-seeing point of view, disturb Huxley no more than the similarly strange diary of Esther Sommerson which shatters the all-seeing texture of Dickens' *Bleak House*. A reader of Huxley's fiction has to resign himself to the likelihood that a consciousness brought to the fore in one portion of a novel is likely to be abandoned for another and more useful awareness.[51]

One can see this defect with particular clarity in the short stories of this period. Short stories would seem to demand more scrupulousness in this matter than long novels, but such attention is often disturbingly absent. One is, for example, halfway through "Happily Ever After" before he makes out that the story belongs not to a visiting American scholar but to the English girl whose lover is killed in wartime.[52] An otherwise very touching story of a day in the life of an elderly and ailing lady's maid, a creature who is cousin to Katherine Mansfield's Miss Brill, is marred by several paragraphs which abandon the awareness of the maid for a bit of domestic conversation between her employers that hardly touches her.[53]

It is just, however, to note that the confusion that mars *Those*

Barren Leaves is mastered in *Point Counter Point,* where Huxley makes an artistic virtue of his roving curiosity; the ubiquity of his point of view is, in that novel, a consistent practice rather than just the distracting snail-track left by an undisciplined attention to complex subject matter. The problem is mastered occasionally in the later novels by limiting the narrative to an account in the style of Francis Chelifer's first-person recollections,[54] or to the consciousness of one character, reproduced in the third-person (thus, nothing is learned in *Island* that Farnaby does not learn).

If one disregards the distracting over-emphasis on the mental history of Francis Chelifer (a poet who has sold his soul for the security of editing a breeder's gazette), one can speak of *Those Barren Leaves* as the development of a metaphor suggested when one of the characters—Miss Thriplow, a calculating and libidinous novelist—plucks some leaves from a bush; they must wither, she realizes, leaving only a faint odor behind them.[55] The novel contains a company of people, some merely laughable and others tragic in the solipsistic sense, people whose experience of life is destined to be a withering, whose experience of love will be that of "parallels."

The hostess of the party is such a detached leaf. Lillian Aldwinkle is a middle-aged woman who uses beauty creams, an uncritical enthusiasm for the past of the villa she presides over, and pursuit of new love affairs to veil her eyes from the reality of aging and personal isolation. She is a Freudian tutor to her niece Irene. Irene —basically a "good" and simple person—is fortunately able to break free of her aunt's sinister wisdom and to plan marriage with an inarticulate, lisping Englishman, who is able to propose only when he is driving a fast car. (The typographical representation of a lisp is, for Huxley, always amusing.[56])

Less fortunate than Irene, more likely to wither, are other members of the party. One of these is Falx, a visiting Labour leader; the formula lying behind his creation is one that often served Huxley well: that of the man whose purposes should add up to emancipation but whose prejudices continue the moralism and even the prudery of past generations. Falx is a second cousin of Shearwater in *Antic Hay* and very nearly blood brother to Illidge in *Point Counter Point.* More important than Falx is Francis Chelifer, who resists Lillian's invitation to a love affair and returns to his breeder's gazette in London; like many another emancipated person in Huxley's fiction, Chelifer avoids love affairs not so much out of conviction as from a sheer repugnance to the sexual act.

Cardan, the elderly Scogin-figure of the novel, becomes involved in a preposterous plan to marry a wealthy moron, Miss Elver, whom he meets with her brother in a hut in the noisome swamplands of the Maremma. Her brother, a reader of Dante, is familiar with the evil reputation of the Maremma; he has brought his sister there, hoping she will die and leave her money to him. Cardan spirits the sister away in a wonderfully grotesque sequence, which is terminated by Miss Elver's death, caused by her untimely greed for a serving of tainted fish. (The presentation of the courtship and death of Miss Elver is a masterfully heartless episode, rivaled in Huxley only by the tale of the seduced nun, "Nuns at Luncheon." [57]) In the Miss Elver section the uncaring satirist is at the helm; there is no stir of sympathy for the exploited idiot—only amusement for the elderly schemer whose plans for a settled future are ended by a surfeit of fish.[58]

There is a weak fruition of love—as much of a fruition as Huxley ordinarily permits his intelligent characters—in the relation between Miss Thriplow, the novelist, and the traveler and connoisseur, Calamy. These two remain behind at the villa while the rest of the company escorts Chelifer's mother and Falx to Rome. Miss Thriplow's love affair is a failure and "withers" because she, like the heartless lady writer who recounts the distressful history of the nun in "Nuns at Luncheon," has a double consciousness: a love affair may move one, but it must also be studied as material for a novel. Because of her pursuit of "material," Miss Thriplow is unable to give herself in love. Additionally, as Huxley makes clear, there must be a "self" to be given in love—and Miss Thriplow can only alternate between poses of worldliness and poses of girlish simplicity. Her poses are analogous to the "beard" with which Gumbril, in *Antic Hay*, seeks to define his shapeless ego.

The affair brings little satisfaction to Calamy, but for a different reason. His consciousness is systematically aware of the solipsism that vexes many later heroes: he recognizes that his relation to Miss Thriplow is a "love of the parallels," for physical embrace has not really united two persons. Calamy is a man committed to the horrible isolation ward of his own nature: his own nature that is, *tout court,* human nature. Calamy attempts to explain to Mary Thriplow why he is so unsatisfactory a lover:

> It's extraordinary . . . what a lot of different modes of existence a thing has, when you come to think about it. And the more you think, the more obscure and mysterious everything becomes. What seemed solid vanishes; what was obvious and comprehensible becomes utterly mysterious. Gulfs begin opening all around you—more and more abysses, as though the ground were splitting in an earthquake. It gives one a strange sense of insecurity, of being in the dark. But I still believe that, if one went on thinking long enough and hard enough, one might somehow come through, get out on the other side of the obscurity. But into what, precisely into what? That's the question.[59]

It is a question that, not surprisingly, Miss Thriplow has little interest in, nor are Calamy's friends Chelifer and Cardan much impressed when Calamy, at the end of the novel, imitates the gesture of a desert monk and isolates himself on a Tuscan hillside.[60] It is rather clear that Huxley himself, in contrast, is impressed, not only by the abyss that isolates but by the something beyond it that may possibly cancel isolation. Calamy is a prophetic figure; from the problem that touches him emerge the main interests of many later characters.

With Calamy's retreat from Lillian Aldwinkle's villa, *Those Barren Leaves* comes to a halt. Neither what Calamy discovers, nor the extent to which his discovery is superior to what the other withering beings of the novel put their trust in, is revealed. But, the effect of the novel makes clear, Calamy is on a better path than that followed by the unscrupulous Cardan, the bruised and cautious Chelifer, and the stupid Mrs. Aldwinkle; his path is one that their own folly closes to them, and it is one which the naïve and "good" persons like Irene and Mrs. Chelifer have no need to follow. It is not surprising that in the next novel, *Point Counter Point,* the figure who follows Calamy's contemplative way is Burlap, a hypocrite and a figure of fun. Huxley's period of comparative irresponsibility, which he looks back on in his foreword to a recent edition of *Brave New World,*[61] is full of such reversals of judgment. A human gesture that has been moving does not preclude the possibility of a destructive analysis of it.

Calamy is, as suggested, a predictive figure. The secret that he is poised to investigate becomes, in many a later Huxley novel, an

open secret, a fully experienced one. By means of such discontinuous transformation of the self, later characters turn their backs on
all that they have been; they sever roots that extend into the soil
of a bad past. By this clean break, they become better creatures,
at the price of canceling what they have been. As transformed
beings, they are—more than incidentally—standard-bearers for
the truths that, for the later Huxley, are ultimate, or fairly so.

That Calamy, so early as *Those Barren Leaves*, represents such
a standard, one may doubt. He is no more than a particular "solution" to the problem of isolation. If the clue offered by the novel's
design may be followed (and one hesitates to push this sort of
trust very far in reading Huxley's fiction), one must say that Calamy is no more central to *Those Barren Leaves* than Francis
Chelifer or even Miss Thriplow. Indeed, if one looks at express
statements about religion and mystical experience that appear in
this decade, he must conclude that Huxley's curiosity about religion, Eastern and Western, was a qualified one.[62] It was qualified
by the suspicion that the quest Calamy was embarking on was,
from many sensible points of view, an impoverishment of his nature, however superior to the compromises of Cardan, Chelifer,
and Miss Thriplow. That the later avatars of Calamy are not barren leaves—are, fecundating in the figure coming from Shelley's
"Ode to the West Wind"—is testimony to explicit decisions and
rejections which are far from Huxley's mind in the 1920's.

The 1920's were, for Huxley, a period of wide-ranging curiosity
about all forms of human life and choice. They were times when
Huxley was unwilling to give assent to fixed views about man,
times when the only inclusive statement Huxley would accept underlined the importance of living life for its own sake.[63] "Do
What You Will" is the title of one of his collections of essays
(1929)—a statement, one recalls, inscribed upon the lintel of
Rabelais's new-fangled abbey of Thélème.

IV   Point Counter Point

Point Counter Point (1928) is, aside from *Brave New World*
(1932), Huxley's most famous work of fiction. It is deservedly so,
even though it falls short of attaining the simple and gratifying
focus of *Crome Yellow. Antic Hay* and *Those Barren Leaves* were
attempts to move beyond the exclusively satiric rendering of some
levels of English life to be found in *Crome Yellow,* to refer to

something besides folly, to do justice to what can be called the tragedy of solipsism. In *Antic Hay,* farce had to undergo temporary evaporations in the presence of tragedies like those of Myra Viveash, Emily, and Gumbril (in some moods). Of *Those Barren Leaves,* one is tempted to ask whether the work belongs to Calamy in his Tuscan hut. If so, only by default. That he seems to do well is a result of his being surrounded by many who do so badly. Although he has the last word, it is not really a decisive one.

Who has the last word in *Point Counter Point?* Philip Quarles, keeper of analytical journals which record his sense of apartness? Rampion the artist, whose apocalyptic visions on canvas go "beyond" Cubism and abstraction more definitely than did Lypiatt's in *Antic Hay?* Or Spandrell, who carries to a point of hysteria the dalliance with the abyss initiated by Coleman, also in *Antic Hay?* Or some other figure? The answer, for *Point Counter Point,* must be: all of these major figures—and none of them.

That *Point Counter Point* achieves this kind of clarity—that it has considerable artistic success—is a result of Huxley's very conscious exploitation of a method that he had used more casually in his earlier fiction: the method of counterpoint. Huxley makes, in this novel, a virtue of the difficult insight of the previous one: that a cluster of human awarenesses does not and cannot create a unity or point to a fixed standard that will resolve their differences.

Huxley drew his clue to the successful form of *Point Counter Point* from counterpoint in music, as the enunciative passage about the music of Bach at Lady Edward Tantamount's soiree suggests.[64] Huxley's devotion to musical expression, his analysis of it in essays and other novels,[65] always moves from the strictly musical problems of mode, construction, and so forth to what the music is "saying." His musical criticism is—by many modern standards—just as "impure" as Huxley's glosses on painting, which also move quickly from questions of technique to perceptions of the moral and social meaning of a canvas.[66]

From Bach's counterpoint—from the musical opposition of one theme to another, from the oppositions of different stages of the same theme—the form of *Point Counter Point* takes its clue. In this novel, diverse human melodies are held in contrasting and suggestive relation to one another. But, if *Point Counter Point* is a fictitious equivalent to Bach's elaborate music, it is also a continuation and intensification of techniques of narrative already inter-

mittently used in Huxley's stories[67] and earlier novels where, as in
the love affair between Calamy and Miss Thriplow, the contrasting feelings involved in a love affair of "parallels" are neatly and
effectively played off against each other. As kisses are exchanged,
Miss Thriplow pursues "material" for her novels; and Calamy discovers that fleshly embrace does not cancel his deathless isolation.

In *Those Barren Leaves* the technique of counterpoint is not
systematically used; it is happened on and then abandoned for
monologue, autobiography, or tedious natural description; but
such deviations seldom occur in *Point Counter Point*. With a masterly confidence, Huxley moves in this novel from one fragment of
disparate human experience to another: from the mind of an old
lecher-artist (John Bidlake) fearful of waning powers and death to
the complacent awareness of his still-vigorous former mistress;[68]
from the mind of a socially irresponsible and "pure" scientist
(Lord Edward Tantamount) to that of a socially committed one
(Illidge).[69] He contrasts the whining thoughts of a neglected mistress (Marjorie Carling) to the guilty thoughts of her lover
(Walter Bidlake), whose sexuality requires the stronger lights
and mad music that he finds with the shameless Lucy Tantamount.[70] Human attitudes in contrast with each other are put in
sharp relief; side by side appear the false spirituality of a critic
named Burlap and *his* Beatrice, who finally shares with him not
beatific vision but his bathtub, and the "honest" sensuality of Lucy
Tantamount, who gives up on the finicky Walter Bidlake and
picks up a foreigner who really knows what sex is (he is, not un-
expectedly, an Italian).[71] Morality and religion appear for the
frauds they are; there is a drunken pervert named Carling who
talks about chasubles (his defect has driven Marjorie to the arms
of Walter Bidlake), and there are the ethical harrumphings of
Philip Quarles' father, who pretends to be working on a book on
democracy but really goes up to London to visit his mistress
rather than the British Museum.[72]

These contrasts are presented with a satiric brilliance that, it
must be confessed, does not wait for an answer; there is plainly no
higher court to which these figures, mounted on a pin, can appeal.
Other passages in the novel, as one might expect, demand attention that moves beyond contempt. Through the novel—but inoperative in it—move two "good," somewhat elderly women: Mrs.
Quarles and Mrs. Bidlake and, in the same class with them, two

young lovers, Polly Logan and Hugh Brockle (analogous to Irene and Lord Hovenden in *Those Barren Leaves*). Also in this class of the inoperative good is Ethel Cobbett, the secretary of the critic Burlap; it is she who puts her head into a gas oven when she is certain that her love will not be requited. Another supplement to the destinies of the sheerly stupid and the inoperative "good" is the career of the Fascist leader, Everard Webley, whose murder is apparently patterned on the murder-for-a-thrill performed by Loeb and Leopold in the American twenties.

There is, of course, a strand of interest that expresses the solitude of the sensitive, intellectual person. In *Point Counter Point,* the strand emanates from the person and journals of Philip Quarles; he, like Miss Thriplow of *Those Barren Leaves*, cannot "live" because life, for him, is the source of ingenious fictions. There is an echo of Miss Thriplow's "chemical compound of all the categories" in Philip's meditation on the art of the novel, which, he judges, might well be a set of variations on a given theme, like Beethoven's Diabelli variations. How is this to be done? "All you need is a sufficiency of characters and parallel, contrapuntal plots." Philip's own solitude is perhaps indicated by the kind of fiction he wishes to write: "Novel of ideas. The character of each personage must be implied, as far as possible, in the ideas of which he is the mouth-piece. In so far as theories are rationalizations of sentiments, instincts, dispositions of soul, this is feasible."

He adds, significantly for himself, and certainly with point for any inclusive consideration of Huxley's body of fiction: "The chief defect of the novel of ideas is that you must write about people who have ideas to express—which excludes all but about .01 per cent of the human race. Hence the real, congenital novelists don't write such books. But then, I never pretended to be a congenital novelist." [73] Quarles is—and one can say that Huxley is—a mediator on the human condition, a tourist among the oddities that the human condition has produced in the past and present. For such a traveler, the journal Quarles keeps is not the irrelevance that Chelifer's autobiographical fragments were in *Those Barren Leaves;* for Quarles' journal contains sharp comment on his own plight and that of other characters in the novel. It is significant that Quarles is represented as deeply dependent on the more natural humanity of his wife, Eleanor, who acts as his "dragoman"

and establishes human relations for him that he cannot set up
himself.[74]

This cast of characters is filled out by other figures who represent extremes, negative and positive, of what the human situation
offers man (as the other characters do not, whatever their folly
and fearfulness). Spandrell, the skater on the abyss, represents
life-denial. Life-affirmation is dramatized in person of an artist,
Rampion; it is also presented in his scarcely less powerful wife,
Mary. To them—somewhat ambiguously, it must be confessed—
the structure of the novel gives the chance to have a telling if not
a last word.

All these characters and unmentioned minor ones are held in
successful tension with one another. Some are offered only the
cold meat of satire and others the warm broth of rather sympathetic attention. The variations in Huxley's attitudes toward his
personages—from satire for Burlap and Illidge to concern for the
solipsistic Quarles, the nihilist Spandrell, and the confident Rampions—are made to seem just executions of the basic design of the
novel, which implies restless motion from one range of experience
to another. Additional meditation on the novel may indeed lead
to uneasy perceptions of startling contrasts of tone and variation
in the author's estimate of different human beings; there are first
and second-rank citizens in Huxley's polis, and there is no need to
treat them alike. But—and this is a relative good—the variation
permeates the book instead of being expressed in sections isolated
from each other, as in the previous two novels.

And, at least for a first reading, the discrepancies between
satiric and tragic estimates of man are concealed by the constant
shock of passage from outright adultery to false spirituality, from
pursuit of scientific truth to pursuit of naked power. In the mode
of satire, human dignity is attacked and shattered, as by the parrot that cries out during a potentially tender moment between
Walter Bidlake and Lucy Tantamount,[75] and by the onslaught of
mortal illness that overtakes the artist, John Bidlake.[76] In the
mode of thoughtful attention is presented the tragic destiny of
Quarles, the man who misses the spontaneous goods of life and is
unable to swerve from the "parallel" he follows even at the illness
of his son.[77] Also in this mode is presented the hysteria of Spandrell, who, outraged by the flaccid sexuality of his widowed
mother, wills to destroy his chance to exist along with every other

one in sight: by conscious corruption of the young, by torture of an aging prostitute, by every outrage he can offer his own sensibilities. He reaches, of course, the extreme of negation in his plotting the murder of Fascist Webley—a murder that is to him particularly piquant in that its execution involves the socially idealistic scientist, Illidge.

The same mode of thoughtful attention renders the figures of Rampion, an artist of lower-class origin, and his upper-class wife Mary. From them radiate the only healing powers in the novel— powers that will be without much effect since the world of *Point Counter Point* is far gone in waste and outright evil. Rampion was brought up by a mother "who had done her best to abolish, to make him deny the existence of all the instinctive and physical components of his being." Because of his uninhibited, aristocratic wife Mary, Rampion had been able to win to "some deeper layer of his being." He profited "from her easy laughter, her excellent appetite, her unaffected sensuality. It took him a long time to unlearn the puritanism of his childhood." But from her he finally learned his "noble savagery." [78] Together they constitute a flickering beacon from which emanates a light that a thoughtful character like Quarles observes but is unable to respond to—the light that urges Spandrell to further devastation.

At any rate, the Rampions serve what one might call a Calamy function in the novel; they offer at least debatable possibilities of wholeness in contrast to the division and incompleteness everywhere else visible. It is interesting that the Rampion gospel is expressed not only in words, but in pictures not unlike those which D. H. Lawrence (the pattern for Rampion) left behind: allegorical and pretentious visions of the human arc traced across the biological muck, visions as full of "message" as the apocalyptic designs of a William Blake. It is ironical that, in terms of event and consequence, Rampion is almost as inoperative as the "good" characters in the novel. He lectures the wasters as they sit around the table at Sbisa's restaurant, where he observes to Spandrell: "You like stewing in your disgusting suppurating juice. You don't want to be made healthy. You enjoy your unwholesomeness." [79] He receives visits from Burlap at his studio, displays his paintings, and rather resignedly explains the meaning of his work.

Of the monstrous prehistoric reptiles in one of his pictures, he says: "The lizards died of having too much body and too little head. . . . But what about mental size? These fools seem to forget that they're just as top-heavy and clumsy and disproportionate as any diplodocus. Sacrificing physical life and affective life to mental life. What do they imagine's going to happen?" Rampion appears as a kind of apostle of undifferentiated life-force or energy when he adds: "I must say, I resent being condemned to extinction because these imbeciles and scientists and moralists and spiritualists and technicians and literary and political uplifters and all the rest of them haven't the sense to see that man must live as a man, not as a monster of conscious braininess and soulfulness." [80]

This omnibus rejection ignores the possibilities that Huxley investigated in his later work: the chance that there can be set up a useful relation among the various labors of "scientists and moralists and spiritualists and technicians and literary and political uplifters." Yet Rampion does not, except through his wife, become really involved in the lives of others; he turns out to be in as great need of a female "dragoman" as the meditative Quarles himself. Perhaps Huxley is suggesting that it is enough for such a man to exist and to utter his truth.

What is his truth? That is, what is this positive sensibility at the center of the novel? Rampion's canvases are full of processions that lead from microbe to man, full of human forms that are epiphanies not of man as he is but of man as he might and should be. This is a vision of wholeness—a vision that is obscured, elsewhere for Huxley, by the "holy face" at Lucca and by the perverted humanity of Pascal.[81] Rampion lives in a world surrounded by people who have denied. There are—the vividly colored visions of Rampion assert—possibilities of reconciliation and adjustment among the confused parts of human life that escape the majority of mankind. Is there any hope that these scales of blindness will be lifted from human eyes?

There is, in the novel, little hope. For there is no mistaking the use made of the figure of Spandrell. Rampion points to an acceptance of life in its complexity, with no part canceled out of deference to some other part. (One of the chief ways in which later Huxley gospels differ from this early version is that acceptance of life in its entirety need not be, as with Rampion and his pictures, an uncritical and omnibus embrace. Rather, it can be discriminating, conscious, and critical.) The figure of Spandrell—and here is a reading that Huxley will not alter—points to many a man's rejection of the chance to live, to be instructed. Such a rejection can be considered a sin. Spandrell's cancellation of himself and everything he touches follows naturally from the solipsism which a man like Quarles endures: Quarles is a thinker, a commentator on life rather than one who lives it. If one tires of the solitary track that is one's apparent destiny and if, like Spandrell, one also despairs because of the "betrayal" of a person dear to one, such as a parent,[82] it is easy to move toward a work of destruction.

The work of affirmation is difficult; most men cannot will the discontinuity with a tyrannical and deforming past that Rampion achieved. The discontinuity cannot turn out to be a return to the values supported by careless common sense and organized Christian religion; this seems to be a pattern that works for the "good" elderly women of the *Point Counter Point* world, but it will not work for anyone else. Mrs. Quarles, for example, lives by a collection of well-arranged lies about what life is. What is left for a Spandrell is some *acte gratuit* such as the senseless murder of Webley. Yet the act serves no purpose: killing a Webley does nothing to alter the course of history and offers no illumination to the questing self. Spandrell's courting of death is, at best, a taunt to the world he has rejected and the abyss that is its only support.

In his last hour Spandrell listens to a Beethoven quartet and sighs: "To me it's the beatific vision, it's heaven." Rampion, who is present, says crossly: "Spandrell wants us to accept this disembodied eunuchism as the last word. I won't. I simply won't." Spandrell's eunuchism has consisted of canceling the rich interplay of life in the name of an entity—the "soul"—which has escaped him. Rampion can only remark bitterly: "This damned soul . . . this damned abstract soul—it's like a kind of cancer, eating up the real, human, natural reality, spreading and spreading at its expense . . . Why should he [Spandrell] find it necessary to replace the real, warm, natural thing by this abstract cancer of the soul?"[83]

Spandrell's determination to be either a demon or an angel has made him waste his chance to exist, Rampion would say, as a man. It is clear, at the end of *Point Counter Point*, that Spandrell, the anti-Rampion figure, has no share in Raskolnikoff's conclusion about *his* murderous deed. Raskolnikoff said to Sonia: "What did I kill? A louse." And Sonia, with an effect of intense clarification, answered: "You killed yourself." There is, alas, no Sonia in *Point*

Counter Point. And, one might add, there can be none in the entire body of Huxley's fiction. The statement is no unnecessary derogation of Huxley's talent, one manifestly on a lower plane than Dostoyevsky's.

Instead, the statement points to an essential fact about Huxley's depiction of human relations in *Point Counter Point* and in all his other fiction: Huxley is unable to depict people in real, effective, and shifting relation to each other. Spandrell—like Quarles, like Rampion in a way—talks only to himself. The "good"—the virtuous mothers and the innocent and indeed vacuous girls of Huxley's fictitious world—cannot ever really be heard by the tragic solitaries at the center of that world; the "good" have no chance to give these solitaries some simple "leading" like that which Sonia offered Raskolnikoff. For the tragic solitaries are impervious to human address. They are, in consequence, unable to hear an illuminating command from another being; they are unable to perform the act that Sonia commanded Raskolnikoff to perform: to go forth into the marketplace to kiss the earth and by that kiss prepare to embrace not some omnibus conception of human life— Rampion's or another's—but humanity itself.

A just estimate of *Point Counter Point* must not overlook its superior liveliness, its sheer and untiring energy. In later novels, Huxley continues to achieve effects of ironic comedy almost as good as Sir Edward Tantamount's slide down the stairs that interrupts his wife's elegant concert.[84] But it must be confessed that in later books this excellence is intermittent; such excellence is interlaced with passages in which dogmatic instruction takes over, and persons *as* persons vanish.

Even in *Point Counter Point,* particularly upon reinspection, the characters do not exist entirely in their own right: they are illustrations of typical attitudes; and they embody—in the instances of Quarles, Rampion, and Spandrell—possible convictions of existence and its meaning. Huxley throughout his writing career warned against the impoverishing effect of conscious system. In *Proper Studies* (1927) Huxley observes, in a summary and quite characteristic way: "The greater part of the world's philosophy and theology is merely an intellectual justification for the wishes and the day-dreams of philosophers and theologians."[85] If his later novels move toward some realignment of man's various capacities—a realignment much more considered and specific than anything Rampion offers—they move with what can only be described as hesitancy; an explicitly fashioned vision of man must not be made at the expense of man. Yet much of Huxley's later work supports an interest that leaves behind Rampion and the novel in which he appears. The later novels become vehicles for the explicit ideas about man that were taking shape in Huxley's mind. Many of them, upon careful inspection, turn out to be dramatizations of Huxley's own hopes for "amphibious man," and they approach the condition of complicated and explicit assertion for which Rampion displays scorn.

CHAPTER 4

Brave New World

A T a time when Huxley was involved in his continuing period-
ical journalism and also in the editing of the letters of D. H.
Lawrence, he published his great utopian novel, *Brave New
World* (1932). The title comes from Shakespeare's *The Tempest*,
where the innocent Miranda exclaims: "O wonder!/How many
goodly creatures are there here!/How beauteous mankind is! O
brave new world,/That has such people in't!" (Act V, scene 1).
The lines in Shakespeare are sufficiently ironical since the "creatures" that arouse Miranda's admiration are mostly scoundrels.
Huxley's use of the phrase deepens the irony, for his world of the
future is one that much modern speculations hope will come to
pass; yet the texture of his imagined world is nearer to nightmare
than to heaven on earth.

Brave New World is, by common acceptance, Huxley's most
celebrated book. From the fairly complex point of view towards
Huxley's work that seems to be most just—that of considering
each work by its esthetic success *and* its power to express aspects
of the twentieth-century cultural situation—a kind of double but
related judgment may be passed. As utopian fiction, *Brave New
World* has great esthetic success; it fuses what one presently recognizes as the dangerous incompatibles of this form into a telling
unity. And the novel is, just as interestingly, a notable record of
uncertainties and hopes proper not only to Huxley but also to the
era in which he writes; in consequence, it can be used as a key to
analysis of the times by persons who regard as somewhat irrelevant to their purpose questions of esthetic success.[1] Both sorts of
judgment must be explored. Furthermore, the novel must be seen
as expressive of the developing opinions of Huxley himself.

I   *Utopian Fiction*

One may commence the first of the two interrelated acts of judgment—*Brave New World* as an artistic entity, as opposed to *Brave New World* as a diagnosis of the kind of world which Huxley and his contemporaries shared—by pointing to the esthetic problems which inhere in the writing of utopian fiction. Much modern fiction has the purpose of reflecting the reality which a writer shares with his readers. The starting-point of a realistic novel is the world as it is, whether the writer be a plodding realist like Arnold Bennett or a student of the deeper levels of experience that we call "psychological" (James Joyce or Virginia Woolf). The point of departure in such a novel is still the real world plus the sensibility of the artist who has written the novel. Sensibility, of course, leads to the transformations of reality that distinguish, for example, the novels of Virginia Woolf from those of D. H. Lawrence; both writers shared a real world, and it is their various modes of viewing reality that produce, in *Mrs. Dalloway* and in *Women in Love*, respectively, fictions that present "real" worlds drastically in contrast. Yet the supposition underlying judgment of these novels is that both *Mrs. Dalloway* and *Women in Love* tell about the world as it is.

With utopian fiction, the problem of achieving esthetic success becomes a much more complicated operation. The realistic novelist, psychological or otherwise, offers his world the flattering or unflattering mirror of his own sensibility. In a utopian novel, another mirror is added; and the process by which reality is transformed is intensified. To the mirror of the writer's individual sensibility which reflects what reality is, there is added another which shows what reality might or should be. In consequence of the refraction and transformation of images, of reality, effected by this double mirroring, utopian fiction always offers to a given reality a complicated alteration. This alteration Huxley effected with full esthetic success only once; in *Brave New World*, the consciously distorted representation of certain current tendencies—faith in science, expectation that material and social progress will coincide —consistently reminds the reader of the real world that Huxley's mirrors are reflecting and yet speaks of the realization in the future of possibilities that are only stirring in the present. In much utopian fiction, the reality of the present, which writer and reader share, is frequently cheerfully sacrificed to the firm and tyrannical outlines of the utopian vision.

Huxley's two other utopian fictions—*Ape and Essence* (1948) and *Island* (1962)—are works that are esthetically unsatisfactory. *Ape and Essence* is inferior simply because of the superficiality with which the utopian task is performed; and *Island*, a more ambitious work, fails to please because the interplay of the "mirrors" —one for reality, one for the author's speculations about reality— does not really take place. Alternating in *Island* are techniques proper not only to representing a real, present world but to conveying utopian vision. In *Island* the world as it is and as it can be are both present but are discontinuously represented; the result is something like the layers of Neapolitan ice cream. In contrast, successful utopian fiction—and *Brave New World* has its position here—manages to blend these two opposed ways of viewing the world. Such fiction creates the sense that these two worlds coexist —indeed, have become one.

A cursory recollection of other utopian fiction can call to mind more failures than successes, if the suggested standard, that of temporary fusion, is acceptable. The vision of the ideal country offered in Sir Thomas More's *Utopia* is a manipulated one and no more; reality, in the sense of a continuation or presence of the early sixteenth-century world hangs above the surface of More's imagined island like an irrelevant mist, and the "should be" or "may be" takes precedence over any "is." In such a utopia, the existing and inescapable nature of man and his reactions—the problems of real human interrelations—are no more than fantasms that uneasily haunt the delineation of the new and better customs of "nowhere." The conditions of life as one knows it—in More's instance, as sixteenth-century men knew it—stand in a nonrelation to the conditions of life as it might well be.

Because of this sort of artistic failure, much utopian fiction seems to be the graveyard of abortive human hope. The forgotten utopias of Ignatius Donnelley and the remembered ones of Edward Bellamy and H. G. Wells are, in their various ways, splendid and touching visions. They are splendid because they offer so much; they are often touching because they record a considerable blindness to what, in strength and weakness, lies in man. The vision is great and may be admired; but the vision is negated, reduced to empty fantasy, by what theologians would call the

"anthropology" which informs many a utopia. The novelist's view
of man determines whether his book will be empty or cogent. Too
many utopian novels have been written by persons who failed to
take into account the mixture of dream, courage, incontinence,
and folly that man has always been and probably always will remain. From More's *Utopia* through Wells' *Men Like Gods* and B.
F. Skinner's *Walden Two,* a distressing limitation is apparent.
These books depict confidently the "shape of things to come"; but
they often offer the reader shadows of men rather than the complex human beings, charged with both hope and perversity, whom
one knows from direct experience.

Thus, the difficult task of the writer of utopian fiction is to
achieve a double faithfulness. He must be faithful to the kind of
knowledge he has of his fellow men and to his vision of a future
time. One cannot say that the novels of Wells and Skinner achieve
this double faithfulness. In these books, precise knowledge of man
seems to be sacrificed to hopes for mankind. Such a sacrifice does
not take place in the novels of Orwell, C. S. Lewis, and Aldous
Huxley—at least, the Huxley of *Brave New World.* All three
writers cherish a view of man that sees him hampered by limitations that are an essential part of his nature. That this is a view of
man which is correct, that these limitations cannot be removed at
some future time, is subject to question; and it may turn out that
the hopes of Wells and Skinner have a firmer basis than either
Orwell or Huxley would concede. If so, it will appear that Huxley
was involved in a faithfulness that was misjudged.

The fictions of Huxley and Orwell, indeed, have been called
"anti-utopias" since both men take a dark rather than a confident
view of the future possibilities of man. But an "altar of hope" is
absent from Orwell and Huxley, not just because they do not in
fact hope very confidently but because it demands the cancellation of what man is, in cheerful deference to what man may be.
Neither Orwell nor Huxley is willing to sacrifice hard-earned
knowledge of what man is (reality) to some scheme, some manipulated vision of what society could well be if, charmingly, man
consented to be different. Neither Orwell nor the Huxley of *Brave
New World* supposes that man has the power to annihilate himself as he is and become a footnote to a system. Man must remain,
whatever the utopian setting imagination provides, the mixed,
striving, inconstant being that he declares, to the attentive mind

of the writer, he is. The utopias of Orwell and Huxley record, therefore, a refusal to streamline whatever knowledge of man they have.

The result of this refusal—and here one narrows his interest to Huxley's refusal and its consequences—is an imagined world of very complicated texture. What man *is*—for Huxley, for his reader —does not hang over the *Brave New World* landscape like a miasmal mist that the strategies of a better society will soon dissipate. What man is—at least, to the extent that Huxley was able to determine—becomes inextricably merged with what man has become in the imagined future, in the year 632 of Our Ford. The result, in *Brave New World,* of this preservation of Huxley's cynically sharp, basically cold estimate of the poor forked creature named man is a work of the imagination that convinces rather than arouses amiable and delusory hope. What Huxley asserted about man in his first four novels is true in its own way. What Huxley asserts in *Brave New World* continues to have the same degree of truth. From this one circumstance comes the power of the novel to delight in a sadistic way, and to horrify; the projected world has been successfully fused with what *is*. Another novelist's view of what is—C. S. Lewis', for example—would result in a very different utopia.

II   Brave New World

Brave New World opens ominously: the reader is taken on a supervised visit to the factory where the unborn or yet "undecanted" citizens of the "brave new world" are in the process of being created—not viviparously, but on the conveyor belts that, in dim antiquity, once carried Ford cars from start to finish on an assembly line. Here the reader sees the creation of beings who will not be individuals but will cheerfully belong to each other. In the famous phrase of the novel: "Everyone belongs to everyone else." [2]

This "belonging" is not in the obvious sexual sense alone, for each child has his prenatal development controlled by scientifically determined admixtures of chemical. (An ill-adjusted person named Bernard Marx has been, it is speculated by his happy friends, damaged by an excess of alcohol administered to his foetus.[3]) After decanting—birth—each person undergoes a process of "conditioning" that makes him a willing consumer of the pleasures of sex and sport and a fearful avoider of the pleasures and tastes that separate men from each other. Particular unnatural tastes for beauty, such as a non-consuming delight in bright flowers, is conditioned out of existence.[4] By a process analogous to the famous experiment of Pavlov, who trained dogs to salivate at the sound of a bell rather than at the "natural" presence of food, children learn to fear pleasures that have no function in a tightly planned world.

Genetic differences in this anti-utopia have been foreseen and dealt with fairly well. By the process of Bokanovsky "budding," not just twins and triplets but as many as ninety-six persons are created from one sperm and one ovum.[5] Diversity of social function demands the existence of different classes—Alpha, Beta, Gamma, and so forth—but submission to the conditions of life proper to one's class is rendered painless by hypnopaedia or "sleep teaching." In consequence, each child grows up thinking that his genetic inheritance and social position are indeed ideal.[6] Each person is incapable of resentment when he observes the lot of others: those who direct the society do not, of course, resent those who take their directions; and those who obey have only pity for their superiors who carry a burden of responsibility that they are free from.[7]

Furthermore, each person is incapable of expressing opinions or judgments of his own since these are, in theory and indeed usually in practice, non-existent; verbal education only prolongs the conformity that already existed on the assembly line along which fetuses pass. As the director of the hatcheries explains to his attentive pupils, the suggestions which each child unconsciously receives create the adult he becomes. The process continues "Till at last the child's mind *is* the child's mind. And not the child's mind only. The adult's mind too—all his life long. The mind that judges and desires and decides—made up of these suggestions." The Director concludes triumphantly: "But all these suggestions are *our* suggestions!" [8] Thus does Huxley face the reader with the problem which has apparently vanished from the imagined commonwealth itself: *Quis custodiet custodes?*—who watches the watchmen?

The materials Huxley draws on for fabricating the utopian element in his novel are clearly the commonplaces of progressive hopes for mankind. In the early twentieth century, religious decay

had removed from the minds of many enlightened men any expectation of a last judgment or of some other kind of divine in-
trusion into human experience. If men were to be saved, if the
human experiment were to be salvaged and rendered more significant than that of the dinosaur, man must cease looking for aid
to some deity he had himself invented in his own image; man
must look to himself or, if not to himself, to the superior members
of his species. These—not deity—can be expected to shape the
destiny of future generations. Such superior persons must decide
what man should become and then—by conditioning, by the ruthless imposition of adjustment to the "right" kind of social structure
—see that all men become what, in the minds of intelligent planners, they ought to be.

These assumptions, as Huxley's satiric verve constantly suggests, are framed in a context of materialist convictions about
what man is. Man is but a complex arrangement of chemical elements, and his proper satisfactions lie in the consumption of other
chemical elements: material pleasures, physical actions that con-
sume his tissues and necessitate the further intake of material
items. Thus, in the novel, man passes his leisure hours in the execution of complex games like Centrifugal Bumble Puppy and
Obstacle Golf;[9] indulges in open and honest sexuality;[10] or flies,
if he is a member of the privileged classes, to any spot on earth in
pursuit of amusement—which turns out to be much the amusement he has left behind.[11] Thanks to social engineering, no one
will be in want; and no one will, in consequence, have any cause
to dream of other possible worlds. All men will have arrived at a
point, itself a utopian one, where they will have no reason to have
utopian dreams. And man's own nature, what we incorrectly call
his "natural" discontents, will have been superseded by the com-
forts and certainties that exist under the sign of the Model T.

Huxley's ironical vision differs from two other notable ones of
our time, E. M. Forster's *The Machine Stops* and Orwell's *Nineteen Eighty-four*, in this respect: Huxley's utopia is assumed to be
one which does its work well; but Forster and Orwell project visions of a future that does not live up to the scientific hopes which
had created it. The irony that lies in the depiction of hopes that
have been frustrated (as in Forster and Orwell) is indeed one
that is easy to grasp. Huxley, instead, wishes to underline the

irony inherent in the absolute success of a scientific-sociological vision.

This particular irony gives the reader the impact of what he and Huxley know man "is" on what (as the architects of the "brave new world" have seen the matter) man should be. Man, as Huxley views him in 1932, is not merely a creature capable of peace, harmony, and perfection under proper conditions; he is a creature marked by confusion, fear, and deathlessly individual awareness. Did Huxley himself conceive man otherwise, the capacities and limitations of man in 1932 would be no more than the irritating mist that hangs at the horizon of much other utopian vision. But what man is in 1932 is a persisting element in what man has become in After Ford 632.

Future man, in Huxley's view, will be dogged by limiting insights that are at odds with the optimistic expectations of Sir Mustafa Mond and other planners. Future man will continue to be a creature who knows that he must die; and no supervised visits of the young to the state crematoria will really dissipate man's sense of his own contingency.[12] No amount of neo-Malthusian drill in the schools will annihilate—at least in a few deviates like Bernard Marx and John, the Savage of the novel—the possibility that man is a creature who, sexually, can choose to exist for a particular other person rather than for everyone.

Bernard Marx, for example, looks at the calm yet rapturous face of a temporary sexual partner; ". . . the sigh of her transfigured face was at once an accusation and an ironical reminder of his own separateness."[13] Nor will the pregnancy substitutes available to women turn out to be entirely satisfactory surrogates for the old, obscene experience of giving birth to children.[14] Visits to the "feelies"—the improved "talkies" of A.F. 632—will not give the same results as emotion experienced and inspected in the separate human heart or soul. And it is doubtful that a drug named "soma" will do more than alleviate tensions endemic to man; it certainly will not cancel them.[15] (Huxley is much indebted to the ancient Hindus in his later work; the borrowed term "soma" is an example of this debt.)

Huxley invents a story that makes these points aptly. After the opening visits to the assembly line that put in place the conditioned glories and securities of the imagined world, Huxley sends through their paces four or five main characters. These well-adjusted persons have such names as Lenina Crowne and Helmholz Watson (Huxley's malice appears in the invention of names which hark back to the chief cultural heroes of the nineteenth and twentieth centuries). There is the shrewd ruler of the "one world," Sir Mustafa Mond. There is the complacent director of the hatcheries. Less happy than these persons is Bernard Marx, perhaps damaged, as has been noted, by an excess of alcohol surrogate at an early stage in his physical development.

Indeed, the behavior of Bernard, stunted in height and hardly a worthy Alpha, is the first crack in the Eden of the future. Bernard yearns for nothing less than a permanent sexual relation with Lenina—a desire that strikes this modest girl as hardly decent. Pursuing his hope, Bernard persuades Lenina to go with him on a visit to an Indian reservation. There they encounter the Savage, John, in whom, finally, center all the disruptive elements of this future world—accurately reflecting Huxley's considered estimate of what man inescapably *is*.

The Savage—Huxley tells us—is the offspring of a "civilized" woman, who many years before had become lost in the Indian reservation; the father of the Savage, as it turns out, is the director of the hatcheries. The mother has shocked both the Indians and her son by her attempts to remain "decently" promiscuous in the uncivilized setting. Over the years, the Savage has learned to read Shakespeare; and in that corrupt author—otherwise known only to the director of civilized society, Sir Mustafa Mond—the young man has discovered models of behavior and feeling that had been edited out of the minds of the conditioned inhabitants of London and elsewhere.

As the Controller, Sir Mustafa Mond, explains, the reading of Shakespeare is dangerous. "Because it's old; that's the chief reason. We haven't any use for old things here." There is no room for tragedy or even for a desire to create works that reflect the vision that had overtaken the Savage in his adolescence—the interplay of life and time and death. In Mond's judgment, tragedy does not arise from man's situation; it once arose from the instability of a particular situation—one that in the new society has been erased: "The world's stable now. People are happy; they get what they want, and they never want what they can't get. They're well off; they're safe; they're never ill; they're not afraid of death; they're blissfully ignorant of passion and old age; they're plagued with no mothers or fathers; they've got no wives, or children, or lovers to feel strongly about; they're so conditioned that they practically can't help behaving as they ought to behave. And if anything should go wrong, there's *soma*." [16] This environment is disturbing chiefly to the rare Bernard Marxes of the happy society—and is doubly so to the Savage, who has escaped all the conditioning that makes the manipulated world a second Eden.

When the Savage is taken back to London as a curiosity, he shocks everyone by kneeling to his father, the director of the hatcheries. Shock and incomprehension become more intense when the Savage refuses to have casual sexual relations with Lenina. Certainly, no one in the "brave new world" understands his grief at the death of his silly mother; indeed, when the Savage falls to his knees grief-stricken, he is guilty of grave indecency, and his sorrow imperils the "wholesome death-conditioning" of the children standing in the hospital ward. The horrified nurse fears what his sobs may suggest—"as though death were something terrible, as though any one mattered as much as all that!" [17] At this point and others, the Savage is an enigma that challenges all the self-evident truths on which the superior society has been built. For that matter, how is the Savage to emerge from the predicament in which he finds himself?

As Huxley points out in an introduction to the novel written in 1946, he saw at the time of writing only two possibilities for the Savage: conformity to the world into which he had been introduced or retreat to his passionate, Shakespeare-sponsored, "uncivilized" ways.[18] The novel actually terminates with the death of the Savage, who has indulged in a *penitente* kind of self-flagellation to curb his lustful desires for Lenina—whom he finally kills because she represents to him all that is evil and yet attractive in sexuality.

In his 1946 introduction, Huxley observes that later years revealed to him that a third possibility existed for the Savage. This possibility came to dominate Huxley's mind as the years passed: "Science and technology would be used as though, like the Sabbath, they had been made for man, not . . . as though man were to be adapted and enslaved to them." Even religion would have its place—the kind of religion, of course, that offers valuable supplements to Christianity if it does not cancel it: "Religion would be the conscious and intelligent pursuit of man's Final End, the unitive knowledge of the immanent Tao or Logos. . . ." And, as to what would be the prevailing philosophy of life—one apparently justifiable in contrast to "system"—Huxley answers: ". . . a kind of Higher Utilitarianism, in which the Greatest Happiness principle would be secondary to the Final End principle. . . ." Had *Brave New World* indeed embodied these possibilities, it would have (in Huxley's later judgment) possessed "artistic and . . . a philosophic completeness, which in its present form it evidently lacks." [19] It is more than incidentally significant that artistic and philosophic completeness are much the same thing and rest on the justice of the ideas expressed rather than on the problems of execution and form that usually go under the heading of "artistic."

At any rate, the Savage could have gone "beyond" or "above" both the conditioned security of London and the simplicities of the Indian reservation. He could have journeyed toward the insights into human capacity which Huxley, as a matter of fact, had not perceived with binding conviction at the time of writing *Brave New World*. But Huxley was, in the early 1930's, a "different person";[20] and, as biographical fact suggests, he was still somewhat influenced by the example of the last D. H. Lawrence, who had advocated a kind of visceral primitivism as the proper counter-irritant to a technologized civilization. The Huxley of 1946 had already said goodbye to D. H. Lawrence and to his kind of gospel in *Beyond the Mexique Bay* (1934),[21] but he did not make any effort to adjust his 1932 account of human possibilities to later insight. *That* explicit effort appears in later utopian and non-utopian novels.

Indeed, one may fancy that *Brave New World* might have collapsed under the burden of the "Perennial Philosophy" which had taken command of Huxley's mind by 1946. The effective tension of *Brave New World* vibrates between the two clearly contrasting poles represented by London and the Indian reservation: the London, an achieved utopian future; the reservation, a confused museum of the past. Huxley tried, in his last novel, *Island*, to show man as struggling to go "beyond" the insights of 1932. This novel, with its more complex utopian problem, is an esthetic failure which is perhaps a reason for being content with the fact that the London of *Brave New World* is scanned and rejected by a fairly simple set of standards.

III *Esthetic Impact*

The esthetic success of *Brave New World* has already been suggested, but it should be underlined by reference to Huxley's earlier work. There are none of the false moves indicative of uncertainty of intent that mar a novel like *Those Barren Leaves*. The opening section in the hatchery employs the device of ironic counterpoint that was also successful in *Point Counter Point*.[22] The mode of farce, so excellent in large sections of *Antic Hay*, finds a proper place in the depiction of the utopian world which Huxley has invented as a parody and intensification of all that is deleterious and threatening to human dignity in modern optimistic speculation. The "feelies," soma, conditioning—with terrific verve Huxley pushes these to their absurd logical extension. There is ample room—in this particular utopian vision—for the "savage indignation" that Huxley may have learned from Swift;[23] for *Brave New World* is Huxley's counterpart of Swift's "modest proposal." The references to sexual drill and modish contraceptive belts are no more out of place than Swift's chilling suggestions about eating Irish children.

In abeyance—and happily, from artistic points of view—is the tragedy of solipsism that is seriously at odds with sheer satiric verve in all the earlier novels but *Crome Yellow*. Bernard Marx is doubtless potentially another solipsist, like Philip Quarles in *Point Counter Point*, and so in his way is the Savage. But the experiences of Bernard and the Savage remain assimilable parts of the general demonstration; they do not flaw the structure of *Brave New World* but intensify it by reminding the reader of what is being deformed and canceled by the efforts of directors like Sir Mustafa Mond.

Nor is there any manifestation of Huxley's tendency in later years to deviate into essay, to sacrifice the novel he is writing to cultural, political, and religious insight. In *Brave New World*, as some critics would say, the object is "rendered" rather than discussed. What discussion takes place occurs in the readers' minds and not in pages that would suspend the onrush of the nightmare that is, within its limits and in a very sinister way, absolutely true.

IV *Symptomatic Implications*

One can have admiration for *Brave New World* as a work of art, but estimate cannot, of course, be limited to the esthetic success just looked at. *Brave New World* is also a work that expresses the twentieth-century cultural situation, as it has been known and experienced within the limits of Anglo-Saxon societies—and perhaps elsewhere. *Brave New World*, like much other work by Huxley, presupposes a certain set of expectations rejected and others reshaped or invented. It may indeed be regarded as a violent defense of and lament for the lapsed dignities of all mankind under threat of scientific encroachment. But it is more modest and more accurate to suggest that the novel is best read as a lament for the lapsed dignities of Protestant man.

These dignities were, as was noted in the second chapter of this book, questioned by the theories of Darwin and by debates about man's relation to God and the moral insights that were supposed to rest on this relation. These movements also had their impact elsewhere, but Anglo-Saxon man was peculiarly defenseless once the biblical sanction of morality and social structure was taken away. Once this was subtracted, what was left? In other cultures in the West, there were structures of church and state, even of sheer rationality and trust in it, that would sustain man. Elsewhere all coherence was not necessarily gone if, in Donne's phrase, the possibility of a confrontation between individual man and his God or (more modestly) individual man and his dignity were put in question.

The alternative to an evil world—in this novel, the Savage's flagellation and death—turns out to be, in Huxley's entire development, only a temporary one. In Huxley's later work, other figures take shape and, directed by the hand of the creator, sketch gestures and assume poses that leave behind the Savage and the book he finally dominates. But as a particular deposit of insight, the novel remains significant and continues to speak to later readers of what it is like to have lost one set of insights and to seek others—seek without taking up solutions offered by facile optimism. Huxley's own search did not, as noted already, conclude with *Brave New World;* it continues in the works now to be inspected.

CHAPTER 5

Five Novels (1936 to 1955)

THE last novels, which extend from *Eyeless in Gaza* (1936) to *Island* (1962), are six in number (the intervening ones are *After Many a Summer Dies the Swan* [1939], *Time Must Have a Stop* [1944], *Ape and Essence* [1948], and *The Genius and the Goddess* [1955]). In itself, such productivity is impressive. One needs to remember, moreover, as one scans these novels, that Huxley in this final and extended period of his life was also producing with some consistency works that may be called his "tracts for the times." [1]

Among these non-fiction works, a most notable one is *Ends and Means* (1937), which contains passages that in substance are interchangeable with speculations appearing in *Eyeless in Gaza*. And *The Perennial Philosophy* (1945) is informed by views of man and his religious life that are very close indeed to points of view that are expressed in narrative form in *Time Must Have a Stop*. There are still later works of non-fiction, such as *Science, Liberty, and Peace* (1947) and *Literature and Science* (1963). In addition, there are two collections of essays: *The Olive Tree* (1936) and *Tomorrow and Tomorrow and Tomorrow* (English title: *Adonis and the Alphabet*) (1956). Finally, there are the two works which are treated in the next chapter: the extended and quite tendentious historical studies of the French seventeenth century: *Grey Eminence* (1941) and *The Devils of Loudun* (1952).

The expenditure of such energy one may regard as an expression of a creative élan moving in various directions from the generative center of Huxley's later work: the mature conviction about man and his possibilities analyzed in the latter section of Chapter Two of this study. The novels not only repeat effects and themes that were treated elsewhere, but passages of speculative prose in the novels sometimes assume proportions that many readers do not regard as welcome. It should be admitted that the novels of

Huxley's last twenty-five years made a demand upon patience that was already threatened in the "fragment" of Francis Chelifer's autobiography in *Those Barren Leaves*. This demand led some readers to think with regret of the relative economy and incisiveness of *Point Counter Point* and *Brave New World*, those works which caught Huxley's mind in a time of instability, poised between what he has called the estheticism of his early work and the commitment and doctrinaire certainty of his later days.

A general recognition of these unattractive characteristics must once and for all be made; it would be monotonous to revive comment on these points whenever a particular novel gives cause. For "beyond" or in contrast to these reservations are recognitions that must be accorded the later fictions of Huxley. In them is the work of a man who is meditating on the central problems of many modern men. To be sure, some readers who were grateful for Huxley's earlier attacks on smugness must have concluded that, in works from *Eyeless in Gaza* onward, Huxley was immersing himself in "solutions" which had at one time been inacceptable. Conscious advocacy of decentralization as the proper response to the dehumanization of mass-culture, revival of aspects of traditional mystical and religious experience to offset skepticism and the emptiness of modern life—these can seem like retreats from the earlier determined rejection of any kind of pretense or nonsense. But it should be kept clearly in mind that adverse judgment of Huxley's later fiction reflects not just a protest against *all* novels of ideas; it is likely to be a protest against the particular ideas that dominate the mind of Huxley in his later life.

I   Eyeless in Gaza

What strikes a reader of *Eyeless in Gaza* at the outset is an artistic form that is, as a very external kind of strategy, unusual. The novel is a succession of portions of the experience of Anthony Beavis and others; each portion is precisely dated, but they do not follow each other in chronological sequence. The reader begins with a fragment of Anthony's experience dated August 30, 1933, and ends with another fragment, dated February 23, 1935. Between these two sections—the first depicting an unsatisfactory stage in Anthony's love affair with Helen Ledwidge and the last representing a resigned reconciliation between the two—are fifty-two other fragments or chapters, each also precisely dated. But the dates of these sections extend as far back as November 6, 1902, the funeral of Beavis' mother. Other fragments include material that indeed falls between the dates noted above.

Furthermore, although the majority of the sections do indeed concern the experience of Anthony—sometimes presented in the third person and sometimes in the form of a journal which Anthony keeps—there are others in which he does not appear. One section, for example, tells how Helen Amberley (Ledwidge) defies her respectable sister Joyce on a shopping tour; Helen maliciously boasts that she will steal something in every shop they enter, even if she has to pick up a slimy kidney in a butcher's shop.[2] Other sections touch briefly on the experience of more peripheral characters, usually in connection with Anthony or Helen; there is, for example, an account of the last day in the life of Ekki Giesebrecht, for a time Helen's lover and, as events turn out, a political martyr.[3] There are, however, sections which leave both Helen and Anthony behind: for example, the one in which Helen's promiscuous mother, Mary Amberley, submits to the contemptuous embraces of her young lover, Gerry Watchett.[4]

Even such fragments finally cast some light—if only by negative contrast—on the decision that Anthony finally makes: to try to follow the gospel announced to him by an anthropologist named Miller. (There are some grounds for judging that the Miller-figure may have been suggested to Huxley by the Reverend Dick Sheppard, an Anglican clergyman active as a pacifist in the 1930's.) In the long run, *Eyeless in Gaza* is not just another *Point Counter Point*, where the center of interest is the fact of the ironic jumble of human experience. Rather, in *Eyeless in Gaza*—the title refers to the rebirth of Samson after the Philistines inflicted blindness and servitude on him—the experiences that are not Anthony's are present not for the contrast they offer all other experiences (as in *Point Counter Point*), but to confirm and oppose Anthony's own particular growth in grace—or so they can be understood. Looking at a collection of old snapshots in the company of Helen, Anthony breaks out: "All this burden of past experience one trails about with one!" He adds: "There ought to be some way of getting rid of one's superfluous memories. How I hate old Proust! Really detest him."[5] A rather ungrateful outburst since the entire novel—particularly as it is arranged—is a kind of collage of sections of Anthony's past and, as noted, fragments not his own that

have their contribution to make to the "present" that finally
enables Anthony to transform the random assemblage into a picture that has meaning for him.

Most of Anthony's experiences—and some of those endured by
Helen—exemplify the insight of St. Paul's: "I see and approve of
the better; and I choose the worse." Anthony notes in his diary:
"Five words sum up every biography. *Video meliora proboque;
deteriora sequor.* Like all other human beings, I know what I
ought to do, but continue to do what I oughtn't to do." [6] Most of
Anthony's life has been a betrayal of himself and other persons—
or has been until he meets Miller in Mexico, where Anthony and
his bellicose friend, Mark Staithes, have gone to take part in revolutionary activity. Miller—a doctor and anthropologist of Quaker
simplicity and directness—teaches Anthony that one's past can be
broken with in the name of a self-discipline drawn from much
religious teaching.[7] Miller observes to Anthony: "We're all of us
what we are; and when it comes to turning ourselves into what we
ought to be—well, it isn't easy." [8] This and much more exhortation finally takes effect on Anthony. Suddenly we see—or at least
Anthony sees—the significance of other events.

Wherever he looks in his past, Anthony can read his basic faith-
lessness to others—to Helen, to his best friend Brian Foxe, and to
Brian's fiancée, whom he has seduced. Other sections of the novel
not directly concerned with Anthony suggest that his record of
betrayal is not peculiar to him. The vice receives ample reiteration
when attention moves from Anthony to Helen or to her mother,
Mary Amberley, who was Anthony's first mistress. Once more, in
this somewhat dreary record of thoughtlessness or deceit, one
finds "the loves of the parallels" that mark the emotional lives of
the clever, self-conscious people Huxley was able to create. A
younger Anthony (May 27, 1914) has already discovered the apparent fact of human isolation and human self-righteousness that
is, one may say, the seed-bed of later betrayals: "That was always
the trouble . . . ; you could never influence anybody to be anything except himself, nor influence him by any means that he
didn't already accept the validity of. . . . the only people anyone ever convinced were the ones that nature and circumstances
had actually or potentially convinced already." [9]

The derangement of ordinary time-sequence at least underlines
a point increasingly important for Huxley: time, though the obvi-

ous medium of human perception, is not worthy of the trust man puts in sequence. The sequence may easily be broken into fragments and reassembled, as in *Eyeless in Gaza;* meaning lies in the rearrangement of events and in conscious assessment of them. Under the guidance of a man like Miller, Anthony at least comes to the conclusion that the essential meaning of his past—negative as that meaning mostly is—must be a cluster of impressions free of the ordinary linkages of before and after. This meaning, created by Anthony's partial triumph over common-sense time, remains ethical and psychological. When Miller engages Anthony and his activist friend, Mark Staines, in conversations, the crucial term in these discussions is sometimes "goodness"; and sometimes they seem to point toward discovery of the various means by which different people can be led toward goodness, toward freedom from hate, toward non-violent action.

Into Anthony's exacerbated awareness of what he is, and what he has done, flow recollections from all the stages of the past—his school days, his more mature friendships, his love affairs. But confession of a fault is not enough; one must will—as Miller suggests —to become what one has not been. Helpful to this act of will is the sort of mystical insight that becomes a main theme in Huxley's latter work: that supporting ethical and psychological wisdom is an inclusive unity. This unity is the beginning and the end; all that lies between is, relative to that unity, evil. Huxley observes of Anthony and of people in general: "The point is that, even with the best will in the world, the separate, evil universe of a person or a physical pattern can never unite itself completely with other lives and beings, or the totality of life and being." Should this isolation, this persistence of solitude, depress one? Huxley advances assurance that would sound strange from him in *Crome Yellow* but that has little effect of oddity in *Eyeless in Gaza*— "Meanwhile there are love and compassion." [10]

If these insights are admired, if it is judged they rest firmly on the narrative context Huxley provides, one may regard the disordered time-sequence of *Eyeless in Gaza* as justifiable. It must be added, as one turns from the ideas the novel expresses to the texture of the novel, that the experiment is executed in a somewhat mechanical way. One cannot see that the style of any particular dislocated section undergoes any alteration because of its unexpected position. Each section is written as Huxley writes quite similar sections in other novels, where they appear in conventional sequential positions. A curious but instructive undertaking is to read the sections of *Eyeless in Gaza* not as they are arranged but in the exact order suggested by the dates that are the chapter headings; no essential meaning is lost.

Significantly, much of the suspense of the novel ebbs because—with the exception of the kidnapping of Helen's German Communist lover in Zurich—the concluding sections in the rearranged sequence are chiefly discourses delivered by Anthony's enlightener, Miller, and accounts of the effort Anthony makes to develop his powers as a public speaker on behalf of pacifism.[11] Huxley's scrambling of time defers to the end of the novel the crucial 1914 experience, the truly great betrayal; at this time Anthony heartlessly and shamelessly seduces Joan Thursley, the fiancée of his stammering friend, Brian Foxe—a seduction that shortly leads to Brian's suicide. This betrayal is the greatest sin he has committed; perhaps it is delayed for this reason to the latter part of the novel.[12] The seduced maiden and the stammering friend are both "good" characters and are projections into this novel of the Emily of *Antic Hay* and the stammering Lord Hovenden of *Those Barren Leaves*. Neither deserves the treatment Anthony's perversity —his inability to divine the reactions of others—allots them; Helen, on the other hand, has a proud solitude of her own and in a sense earns what she receives from Anthony; her suffering at his hands appears in the opening sections of the book.

Issues of arrangement to one side, how is one to estimate the effect of Anthony's experience, moving from unprofitable or mistaken contacts to the illumination that comes to him when he meets Miller? This experience is, par excellence, Huxley's version of the "apprenticeship" novel (*Bildungsroman*)—a type of novel as old as Goethe's *Wilhelm Meisters Lehrjahre* and one exemplified in numerous Victorian and Edwardian works—such as Dickens' *Great Expectations*, Meredith's *Ordeal of Richard Feverel*, and E. M. Forster's *The Longest Journey*. *Eyeless in Gaza* is, one has the impression, the novel Huxley was on the point of writing ten years earlier when he constructed the autobiographical fragments attributed to Francis Chelifer in *Those Barren Leaves*. But in that novel the "apprenticeship" to life of Francis Chelifer is not fulfilled since he merely retreats from the embraces of Lillian Aldwinkle and Italy—retreats to the safety of a breeders' gazette and does not undergo changes of attitude that would amount to either a rejection or a reinterpretation of his cynical past. Such a rejection and reinterpretation Anthony Beavis effects, in the process of meditating on those sections of time that are finally instructive to him.

The portion of his life that tells for him begins with the death of his mother and his growing sense of a lack of communication with his father—first sunk in grief and then cut off from his son by a second marriage. (Here one is reminded of Spandrell's more intense reaction to his mother's second marriage in *Point Counter Point*; the covert sexuality of one's elders is always a kind of betrayal.) Events of his school years intensify Anthony's solipsism, the ultimate tragedy for a Huxley hero. The crassness and cruelty of the boys thrust him into studies that, many years later, result in the sociological and ethical ruminations that the reader samples.[13]

Three boys from this early time figure in Anthony's later years. There is Hugh (Goggles) Ledwidge, who becomes the husband of Helen, Anthony's mistress. A second school friend is Mark Staithes, in his youth a bully and in his manhood an espouser of violent causes for no other reason than that they are violent; he begins as a kind of Steerforth (out of Dickens' *David Copperfield*) and goes on to be a diminished Spandrell. Like Spandrell in *Point Counter Point*, Mark fears the abyss of nothingness which only a cause, *any* cause, and feverish activity, no matter how destructive, can fill. To one of Miller's probing questions—"Is danger your measure of goodness?"—Mark answers, with almost the accent of a Hemingway hero: "What is goodness? Hard to know, in most cases. But at least one can be sure that it's good to face danger courageously." [14] All that Staithes has to show for his pursuit of action for its own sake is, at the end of the novel, the loss of a leg incurred during a trip to Mexico; he had intended to take part in a revolution there, a revolution that interested him chiefly because of its probable violence.

The third school friend is of course Brian Foxe, whose stammering sympathy makes a partial breech in Anthony's isolation and who, together with his "good" mother, gives Anthony an occasional sense of being in touch with other persons. But Anthony destroys this valuable bridge between himself and another human being; as noted, Anthony seduces his friend's fiancée and is the cause of his friend's suicide. Anthony tries to place the blame on Brian's mother: "She had been like a vampire, fastened on poor Brian's spirit. Sucking his life's blood. . . . Yes, a vampire. If anyone was responsible for Brian's death, it was she." [15] But, although Anthony sees through his self-justification, his insight does not keep him from many later falsehoods about himself.

These three persons and a crew of minor figures, who often seem to be on a visit from *Point Counter Point*, comprise the social universe which is physically present to Anthony but to which he does not really belong. For some time he is the lover of Mary Amberley, a woman older than he; heartless, gay, and witty, she introduces him to physical love but to little else. But her daughter Helen Ledwidge offers Anthony the opportunity of loving a person as well as an amorously deft body; he rejects the chance. Out of fear of the demands a complete relation makes? Out of a desire to protect the isolation that allows him to achieve cold excellence in his intellectual tasks? Both questions point to affirmative answers. But, by withholding himself, Anthony betrays Helen as, years earlier, he had betrayed Brian Foxe.

Anthony's behavior, however, does not involve him in a betrayal of his former schoolmate and Helen's husband. Hugh Ledwidge is a second-level character whose impotence and whose Shelleyan romanticism are treated with contempt by Huxley. One should note that Huxley to the end of his career peoples the background areas of his novels with persons to whose shortcomings he offers no more sympathy and comprehension than, at the outset of his career, he offered the eccentrics of *Crome Yellow* and *Antic Hay*. The failure of sympathy is a more signal defect than the technical confusions contained in the later novels.

This defect must be carefully noted in any final estimate of Huxley as a novelist. For there is a lack of consonance between the attention given the central (and solipsistic) figures like Anthony and the cold indifference for figures like Ledwidge, who are beneath contempt and are useful only as figures in the hellish landscape through which persons like Anthony and Helen wander. Indeed, Huxley's infernal visions are peopled by grotesques like Hugh. From such petty monsters can come no guidance to a better life. Their feeble claim to humanity offers no clue to the self-conscious solipsists on whose destinies Huxley broods.[16]

If not from Hugh, if not from an equal like Helen, from what source does come help for a man like Anthony? Whence the wisdom that does enable him, in the latest years of his experience, to move outward toward others and towards society—to move, it is true, awkwardly and with the touching determination of someone who is learning a process (relation with others) that should be as natural as walking? There are two chief sources of help to Anthony. (A third source, that of spiritual illumination, bulks large in several of the remaining novels; but it is not important in *Eyeless in Gaza*.) The first source of help is simply that meditation on the past which has been noted. It is finally in Anthony's power to choose the good and avoid evil.

From this power, beneficent results ensue; Anthony and Helen begin to live together again. Anthony even shows respect for Helen's dead German lover who, earlier, would have been beyond his capacities of response. When Helen remarks sadly that she was not "carrion" in Ekki's company and doubts that she can sustain the sense of dignity she once briefly had, Anthony kindly remarks that she can sustain the attitude she learned from the dead man: "It's a matter of choosing. Choosing and then setting to work in the right way." [17] The utterance expresses a degree of kindness that Anthony, in his earlier days with Helen, did not command.

A second source of change for Anthony is the contact already noted: the acquaintance with the anthropologist Miller, whose discourses on the necessity of pacifism,[18] whose practice of non-violent defense of a cause,[19] and whose self-reliance during the amputation of Mark Staithes' leg in Mexico[20] give lessons to Anthony. Anthony judges Miller to be a man who seeks out contacts with others and has no fear that these will weaken him. Miller, in this novel, is a guide to a fuller humanism than Anthony could discover by himself. He is but one of the gurus—teachers and enlighteners—that are to be found in Huxley's fictions. Perhaps the first of these was Rampion, the D. H. Lawrence figure in *Point Counter Point*, whose insight is expressed by angry, somewhat undiscriminating pronouncements: "To be a perfect animal *and* a perfect human—that was the ideal." "It was a duty not to be a barbarian of the conscience." [21] Sentences like these sum up Huxley's view of Rampion's message, spoken *and* painted.

Miller does not encourage Anthony to cancel the intellect; he puts before him models of its better use, such as the Tibetan injunction: "Constantly retain alertness of consciousness in walking, in sitting, in eating, in sleeping." [22] From the mind's control over all the actions of the body, as Eastern yoga suggests, come harmony and control more refined and directed than displayed in Rampion's pursuit of "life." Anthony makes this estimate of the "way" that Miller has revealed to him: "A method of achieving progress from within as well as from without. Progress, not only as a citizen, a machine-minder and machine-user, but also as a human being." Thanks to proper, conscious direction, it "becomes easier to inhibit undesirable impulses. Easier to follow as well as see and approve the better. Easier to put good intentions into practice and be patient, good-tempered, kind, unrapacious, chaste." [23] The last word would have aroused Rampion's anger, with its overtones of a stunted sexuality; but, by the time of *Eyeless in Gaza*, Huxley had clearly defined his own attitude: an undiscriminating sexuality is not a means to human growth.

Anthony's years of learning have extended to the age of forty-three, practically Huxley's own age when he published the novel. Whether by design or because of a continuing lack of Huxley's, Anthony's emergence from solipsism is incomplete. Like Quarles in *Point Counter Point*, Anthony would still rather meditate than act. And, like Quarles and a considerable company of other characters, Anthony continues to have a fastidious distaste for the physical unattractiveness of many of the human beings who, at Miller's inspiration, he is trying to redirect. (One is reminded of Huxley's own unsympathetic reactions to the Guatemalan "natives" in the almost contemporary travel book, *Beyond the Mexique Bay*.[24]) For Anthony, mankind continues to stink; the inevitable sexuality of man continues to attract his attention and at the same time repel it.

In one of the most symbolic incidents Huxley ever contrived— and Huxley is wonderfully fertile in the invention of incidents that deflate human pretensions—he projects his own and Anthony's distaste for the human lot, particularly for the sexual aspect of mankind.[25] This distaste finds expression in an incident already noted; fairly early in *Eyeless in Gaza*, Anthony and Helen are making love in the daylight on the roof of their Mediterranean retreat. An airman passing over them—incredible detail!—casts out a dog whose body falls on the roof near the lovers and splatters them with blood. The blood does not congeal, as Lawrence might have suggested if he had been writing the passage, but sends Helen away from her lover and sickens Anthony himself with the whole process of lovemaking. For Anthony, the nauseous incident defines the true nature of the desire that he cannot cancel. Man's physiological being—completed in the discharge of semen as well as by the movement of the bowels—is an unworthy joke which the creator, or perhaps only the life-force, has played on man. The human spirit, as a second century Gnostic might have put the matter, has been trapped in a net of filth and couplings from which it would be wonderful to escape. As a Gnostic might go on to suggest, an inferior and even malicious deity—the demiurge—has given man his body. This portion of man eternally wars with the superior deity which has given man his intellect. Huxley's great contemporary, W. B. Yeats, stated Huxley's problem frankly: "But love has pitched his mansion in/The place of excrement. . . ." [26] Yeats was not disturbed by this observation of fact; Huxley was.

Indeed, for a novelist who has written so much about the sexual relation, Huxley has a low estimate of it—although there are passages in *Island* which try to take a more balanced view of the mechanics of generation.[27] Usually, however, the sexual relation emerges as ridiculous and obscene—as unworthy of the being who, it often seems, has no choice but to submit to it. Important for Huxley is the sad case of Jonathan Swift, whose supposed sexual coldness is linked with a "hatred of the bowels." [28] That Huxley shares this hatred to some extent is fairly clear, despite perfervid denials. It is testified to, in *Eyeless in Gaza*, by the halting sexual histories of Brian Foxe and Hugh Ledwidge:[29] histories that have their anticipation in Walter Bidlake's queasy affair with Lucy Tantamount in *Point Counter Point*,[30] in Emily's experience of matrimony in *Antic Hay*,[31] and elsewhere. The ostensible reason that Brian does not marry Joan Thursley is that he is unwilling to let his "good" mother support them, but a deeper reason lies in his repugnance toward the sexual drive itself. Surely the physical need is unworthy of the ideal love he feels—thinks he ought to feel—for his fiancée, whose fornication with Anthony is in large part Joan's response to the desire which Brian has aroused in her and refuses to satisfy. And Hugh Ledwidge's adult sexual difficulties are, one judges, but a continuation of the self-abuse that marked his years at Bulstrode;[32] he cannot satisfy Helen and

writes an evasive, ridiculous book, *The Invisible Lover*, of
"Galahad-like spirituality." [33] Hugh's idealization of love is an
evasion of it; recollection of the book and its author's failures in
bed move his former wife, Helen, to hysterical merriment.

And those characters in this novel and elsewhere who do not
feel the repugnance are just creatures in rut; Mary Amberley and
Gerry Watchett are two of these. Driven by the need for orgasm,
these persons retire from a party for a renewal of the pleasure that
is stronger than the hatred and the boredom they feel for each
other.[34] Finally, a passage in which Gerry seduces Helen suggests
that the usual prelude to intercourse is a selfish, calculated manipulation of the physical desires of the other which flutter like
"moths";[35] the aggressor, at least, has reduced his victim to a ma-
nipulable object. (This scene is in large part a duplication of an
earlier one in *Antic Hay* in which Gumbril holds the simple Emily
in his arms and similarly plays on her inevitable reactions.[36])
Helen's abortion in Paris, sordid in its every detail,[37] is but the
proper consequence of her relation to Gerry, sordid in *its* every
detail.

How is this vein in Huxley to be estimated? Is it puritanism and
prudery masquerading as frankness and open-minded acceptance
of sexuality? Or is the repugnance a by-product of the arrogant
isolation and intellectual pride manifested by many a chief figure,
isolation and pride that cannot but regard natural necessities as a
betrayal of what the superior person would like to be? Possibly.
The question, at any rate, is not resolved until much later
novels.[38] Even in *Island* (1962), where there is what appears to
be a wholehearted endorsement of the sexual act and excretion,
one cannot avoid observing that Huxley has the air of clenching
his teeth and of making the best of a bad bargain between man
and the flesh. This compromise man would never have chosen but
must come to accept.

At any rate, the kingdom of heaven enjoyed by characters in
modern novels who find in intercourse the obvious crown of all
that they are is not one that Huxley's heroes enter with any confidence. They have the air of inquiring: "Must I be involved in
this?" The best that Huxley can do for them is to reply: "Yes,
under certain circumstances." It must be added that, in *Eyeless in
Gaza*, the circumstances are not yet clearly defined.[39]

II   After Many a Summer Dies the Swan

Eyeless in Gaza has, for its conclusion, an acceptance of many of the conditions of life and of action. Under the tutelage of Miller, Anthony Beavis overcomes his tragic isolation and becomes capable of a kind of humanism, a kind of concern for his fellow men. Unlike *Eyeless in Gaza, After Many a Summer Dies the Swan* (1939) is a denial that such concern, such immersion in the ordinary and immediate preoccupations of men, is anything more than an interim and unsatisfactory answer to the challenge that comes to the superior person. That person stands reluctant at the edge of a pond where the repulsive, iridescent scum on the surface promises worse horrors to be encountered by him when he abandons his superiority and tries to make some change in the pond. Anthony's experience of time teaches him what it costs to be human. But a still better lesson emerges from the sharper estimate of time itself that is effected in *After Many a Summer Dies the Swan.*

This lesson concerns what it is to be more than human, to rise above the perceptions of one's common humanity, to strive to be more than the single person, the isolated self or identity. The pages of the novel initiate a theme that can seem to be either a celebration of man's ultimate and noble destiny (that of saying a qualified no to the human personality, the self, and history) or a repulsed turning aside from man (his animal nature, his almost ineradicable hypocrisy). Huxley—chiefly in the words of William Propter in this novel—insists that this turning aside, this discarding of time and all that man has learned in time, employs insights that great religious teachers announced long ago.

Propter, an American counterpart of Miller in *Eyeless in Gaza,* expounds his doctrines to any willing listener: "Time and craving . . . , craving and time—two aspects of the same thing; and that thing is the raw material of evil." When his auditor, a young scientist named Peter Boone, objects that potential good is also located in time, Propter replies intransigently that it is only potential evil that is in time, whereas potential good is not. Somewhat dauntingly he spins out sentences like these: "The longer you live, the more evil you automatically come into contact with. Nobody comes automatically into contact with good. Men don't find more good by merely existing longer." His conclusion is, briefly, that "Actual good is outside time." [40]

Assertions like this one make clear that Propter is continuing and expanding themes that were dear to Miller, to Anthony Beavis in *Eyeless in Gaza*—and, finally, to Huxley; they begin to stir outside the novels as well as within them. They constitute the "ends" in Huxley's analysis of the problems man faced in the 1930's: *Ends and Means*.[41] They are made even more explicit in a work of the next decade, *The Perennial Philosophy* (1945). Particularly in the latter book one finds that man's ultimate duty is to escape the tyranny of time, of sequence, of fear for the death that puts a terminus to this sequence—and that the only true philosophy lies in going beyond philosophy. Human fabrications and systematizings in the name of part of the nature of man, the "amphibious being," [42] must have a supplement. This supplement is the direct experience of wholeness which the great religious teachers have all described and which every living man, if he but chooses, can experience.[43]

That man must deny the world of common sense and physical appearance—or put it in some kind of abeyance—if he is to move to another and better range of experience is a contention that takes shape in *After Many a Summer Dies the Swan*. One way that will serve is the *via negativa*, the cancellation of "normal" interests, that religious innovators and mystics have described. Propter puts the matter thus:

If he [man] serves any ideal except the highest—whether it's the artist's ideal of beauty, or the scientist's ideal of truth, or the humanitarian's ideal of what currently passes for goodness—he's not serving God: he's serving a magnified aspect of himself. He may be completely devoted; but, in the last analysis, his devotion turns out to be directed toward an aspect of his own personality. His apparent selflessness is really not a liberation from his ego, but merely another form of bondage.[44]

This directive makes less central to human improvement the ethical and psychological lessons that Anthony drew from Miller's teaching; someone who takes Propter seriously must make a cleaner sweep of the self than Anthony had to make.

At the center of *After Many a Summer Dies the Swan* is, as

noted, a man named Propter. He is a Rampion who has rejected painted allegories for explicit statement; a Calamy (of *Those Barren Leaves*) who no longer seeks answers but possesses them; a Miller (of *Eyeless in Gaza*) who knows that concern with suffering bodies and confused modern morality and politics is not enough. Beyond these relatively worthy concerns of earlier Huxley enlighteners move Propter's own visions. These visions of what man may become are chiefly addressed to Pete Boone who, with his concern for scientific knowledge and for the outcome of the Spanish Civil War, is a variant of Illidge in *Point Counter Point*. Propter sees chances for an improvement of all men that has for apex the emergence of a relatively small number of truly superior men—superior because they do not solve their dilemmas by sinking back into animality or by exaggerating to themselves the accomplishments of human reason.

The superior person—and what he is able to conclude and to experience is important for all men—will move beyond the self that seeks realization in time and toward what Propter calls, with some embarrassment, "the level of eternity" or even God.[45] A superior man ceases to ask certain questions because he knows that the strictly human personality, the isolated self, is not a reality but a fiction which men cobble together to hide from themselves the fact that, in time, man is just a succession of states, of discontinuous gestures. Such isolated states and moments cannot possibly constitute a unity. The self and the personality which people talk about at length are but façades that men erect to conceal from themselves their lack of wisdom.

Wisdom, as Huxley keeps saying with an accent common to much Eastern religion, is the product of a special kind of compassion and understanding: compassion for the folly that leads most men to speak of *their* separate destinies, understanding that perceives these separate destinies as infinite variations on one destiny. The wise man, unlike his benighted fellows, ceases to love—with possessiveness, with attachment—other human beings, as well as other entities such as property, political parties, religious institutions, the nation, or science as a self-sufficient activity. Only a man who has ceased to love in the ordinary fashion, who has ceased to be deeply concerned with the sharp distinctions that go by the name of *good* and *evil*—only such a man can be of use to other human beings.

This kind of man has immersed himself not in a society (as Anthony Beavis mistakenly did, in *Eyeless in Gaza,* under the direction of Miller); for there is, one might say, a better immersion. Beyond time and all that takes place in time is a being or an entity; this being or entity is devoid of personality, cannot "love," and is indifferent to the good and evil on which ordinary human desire centers. Propter can only look with a kind of gentle sadness at a generous young man like Peter Boone: "There was native intelligence there and native kindliness; there was sensitiveness, generosity, a spontaneous decency of impulse and reaction. Charming and beautiful qualities! The pity was that by themselves and undirected as they were by a right knowledge of the nature of things, they should be so impotent for good, so inadequate to anything a reasonable man could call salvation." [46]

Propter is such a reasonable man; Huxley presents him as enjoying a freedom denied all the other characters in *After Many a Summer Dies the Swan.* Propter works for others in practical ways; he resists the exploitation of the Oakies by his wealthy friend, Jo Stoyte, and speculates about the possibility of reducing the vertigo of mass culture. But he does these good works with non-attachment. He will not work for man as Peter Boone worked when he risked his life for the Loyalist cause in Spain. Barcelona will fall, and so will other cities that are brick and mortar expressions of transient human desires. To work for human good is not (Propter indicates) to work for goods that men ordinarily call "good." It is to work to establish the preconditions of vision in as many men as possible; but vision, of course, is not possible for very many men. As *After Many a Summer Dies the Swan* suggests, the world is peopled chiefly by persons who have no desire to experience insights that are independent of time. The few who do move toward such insights unconsciously resist them or forget them or, like Peter, are senselessly killed when they are on the verge of discovery.

Propter does in fact support a kind of sketchy social program as, one might say, the precondition of vision. He censures Jo Stoyte, the wealthy man of the novel for paying the Oakies wages that will not allow them ever to forget the pangs of physical hunger. (Stoyte is obviously patterned upon the journalism magnate, William Randolph Hearst; and the pleasure-palace of the novel has links with Hearst's California mansion, La Casa Grande. The

Oakies at least seem to come from the pages of Steinbeck's *The Grapes of Wrath*, which was published some months before Huxley's novel.) Because Propter also censures the imposition, in southern California, of a mass culture that deadens a person's ability to reflect, he is out of sympathy with Stoyte's endowment of a culture center and university called "Tarzana," and feels only pity for Stoyte's own castle, stocked with plunder from European civilization that ranges from boxes of documents in the basement to Vermeers in the elevator. And Propter does little to encourage his friend Peter's infatuation with Virginia Maitland, the lovely, empty girl who plays, for Jo Stoyte, the roles of both mistress and daughter. It is clearly Propter's conviction that only the person who has ceased to love humanly—ceased to single out *one* being as an object of love—has reached the position where his mind can be aware of the nameless, passionless deity or nullity that is "there" for him to know.

Propter's only explicit panacea is decentralization of industrial production; he supervises a little cottage-industry in his own house.[47] (Amusingly, he is able to do so because he has had an inheritance.) He is, however, more deeply concerned with what some of the sciences can tell him about the unused capacities that exist in man.[48] These capacities can be used by persons who are trying to move forward a little way from the unreflective human condition. Clearly, Propter, like Huxley, has little use for the pursuit of knowledge of any sort for its own sake. The library and the laboratory in Jo Stoyte's castle are indeed potentially creative places and could be the scene of discoveries useful to man; but they can also become places of cowardly, irresponsible refuge, where the scholarly or scientific ego imitates Narcissus. The only human being who is truly free is the person whose fancy has not been caught by the playthings of the body (Virginia Maitland) or by those of the mind, and thus is not a slave to time, whose creations these playthings are.

Propter unequivocally subscribes to the view that indulgence in sexuality is not morally wrong but just strategically inexpedient for the man who wants to end his servitude to time. Avoidance of sexual relations opens the way to other relations. Love, on the human level, in Propter's view, "stands for a great many different states of mind and ways of behaving. Dissimilar in many respects, but alike at least in this: they're all accompanied by emotional excitement and they all contain an element of craving. Whereas the most characteristic features of the enlightened person's experience are serenity and disinterestedness. In other words, the absence of craving." [49] Sexuality was for St. Paul one of the chief means by which the devil enslaves man; for Propter-Huxley, it is one of the chief means by which the imagination of man is kept within the terrible limiting context of time.

This account of Propter's ideas, delineates not only Propter but most of the Propter figures in still later novels.[50] Such delineation of Huxley's hopes for man—hopes for which he is determined to propagandize, whatever the cost to his novels esthetically—indicates his willingness to endanger the *art* of his fiction. Peter Boone, for example, hears baboons gibbering and is painfully reminded of what Propter has said about literature: "About the wearisomeness, to an adult mind, of all those merely descriptive plays and novels, which critics expected one to admire. All the innumerable, interminable anecdotes and romances and character-studies but no general theory of anecdotes, no explanatory hypothesis of romance or character." There is, in even the greatest literature, "no co-ordinating philosophy superior to common sense and the local system of conventions, no principle of arrangement more rational than simple esthetic expedience"—a stricture that, incidentally, goes far to explain the particular texture of Huxley's own fiction, which progressively moves toward the subordination of esthetic effect and verisimilitude to a "co-ordinating philosophy superior to common sense and the local system of conventions."

The prime defect of the very greatest literature is, in Propter's view, that "it took seriously the causes of suffering as well as the suffering. It helped to perpetuate misery by explicitly or implicitly approving the thoughts and feelings and practices which could not fail to result in misery." Significantly, only satire can sever man's interest from the constricting web of passion and hope that holds him back from deeper perception; therefore, ". . . a good satire was much more deeply truthful and, of course, much more profitable than a good tragedy." [51] Satire—as Huxley sees the art and as many other satirists do not—points beyond the constricting web. Other works of literary art remain the daughters of time and cannot help the man who wishes to become the child of infinity.

Plainly, this judgment of literature and, by implication, of other art is not likely to please a century such as the twentieth—in which art is one of the few remaining foci of value. But Propter, in his dismissal of "the best that has been thought and said," is not urging on Peter Boone, a young scientist, the study of the humanities: "The best that has been thought and said. Very nice. But best in which way? Alas, only in form. The content is generally deplorable." He adds: "Insofar as we think as strictly human beings, we fail to understand what is below us no less than what is above." [52] Man, the "amphibious animal," must have mastery of what is below him, and on this the practicers of humane letters are generally agreed; but man must also pursue mastery of the mystical vision which lies beyond rationality and the arts it has fashioned; and about this pursuit—Propter is sure—the very greatest creators of literature and other arts have had little to say.

Structually, Propter is at the center of the book and has more nearly a dominating position than Miller in *Eyeless in Gaza*. Even so, the novel begins as the account of an experience that belongs to Jeremy Pordage. Dominating the early part of the novel is Jeremy's introduction, as a dazzled English intellectual, to the slogan-spangled highways of California, to the cemetery owned and exploited by Jo Stoyte, and to Stoyte's own fantastic castle. (It is that section of California that Huxley first sketched in his travel-journal, *Jesting Pilate*,[53] and that furnished Evelyn Waugh with an entire novel, *The Loved One*.) Jeremy's instructed and cynical reactions are supported, at a distance, by those of his elderly mother, to whom he stands in a mildly incestuous relation. (Mrs. Pordage is one of the few parents in Huxley's fiction who are as un-"good," as disillusioned, as their offspring.)

Yet, as one should expect by now, Huxley is not bound by his useful opening gambit: the exploitation of Jeremy's English consciousness. Huxley is obliged, in a kind of service to Propter's insights, to turn away from Jeremy's amusement to more passionate human aspirations; in them, not in the cynicism of a man like Jeremy, lurks the cancer at the heart of human effort. The most sinister malignancy in the novel is that to be seen in Jo Stoyte, the wealthy man whose thirst for continued life, for continued experience of time, is sharply at odds with Propter's relative indifference to the gifts of time. These gifts are, for Stoyte, represented by his palace where the artifacts of Rome, Medieval Spain, and Renaissance Italy are jumbled together in a meaningless confusion. This lack of discrimination on the esthetic level is anal-

ogous to the moral confusion that allows Jo Stoyte to be, on one
hand, an exploiter of Oakie labor and of the general human fear
of death that underwrites the success of the ridiculous cemetery
and, on the other, a tender lover of Virginia Maitland and a
coward himself in the face of old age and death. None of his emotions, alas, teach Stoyte anything about the emotions of others; his
love for Virginia does not allow him to forgive and understand the
young scientist's love for her, and the fear of death never leads
him to question his cemetery profits that come from other persons'
similar fears.

This fear of death causes Stoyte to endow the scientific re-
searches of the Levantine Dr. Obispo[54] into the entrails of carp
and their longer-than-human life. The fear of death, of cancellation as a person, as well as ordinary jealousy, causes Stoyte to kill
Pete, the young scientist, who he imagines is Virginia's lover. Actually, the Levantine Obispo has played this role and has reduced
Virginia to a congeries of animal reactions by a sexual engineering
reminiscent of Gumbril's exploits in *Antic Hay* and Spandrell's in
Point Counter Point.[55]

The plot of the novel, often interrupted by Propter's preachings
to Pete (who listens) and to Jeremy (who does not), is amusing
and justifies a characterization of the novel as picaresque; there is
a mélange of loosely connected incidents quite unlike the serious
representation of the work of time in *Eyeless in Gaza*. Particularly
in summary—less so in actual reading—the events of *After
Many a Summer Dies the Swan* have the air of being satirically
conceived and handled. Jeremy is a British scholar who has been
brought to California to inspect a collection of papers owned by
Stoyte. These are the Hauberk papers, the detritus of the many
generations of a noble British family. In the course of his investigations, Jeremy discovers a diary in which the Fifth Earl prolongs
his life into the nineteenth century by eating the entrails of carp, a
detail that arouses Dr. Obispo to heights of scientific enthusiasm.
" 'Christ!' said Dr. Obispo, unable to contain himself any longer.
'Don't tell me that the old buzzard is going to eat raw fish
guts!' " [56]

After Stoyte's murder of Pete, the magnate, his mistress, and
Obispo journey to England. Stoyte goes to escape the consequences of his crime; Virginia, to continue to enjoy Obispo, the
lover she hates (the usual passional ambivalence in Huxley); and

Obispo, to verify suspicions he has formed: that the Fifth Earl of Gonister is still alive in subterranean caves beneath the house where he once lived. Obispo's suspicions are quickly justified. The Earl and his housekeeper are discovered in dank, stinking cells, where they enjoy something like eternal life. This life is thoroughly nasty and brutish (in Hobbes' phrase), if not short, for the "immortals" have developed a profound, anthropoid senility which is hideously underscored when the Earl urinates in the presence of his unknown visitors and then retires to the back of the cave to copulate with his withered female companion.

This scene—in terms of both plot and theme—is the answer to Stoyte's hope that Mrs. Mary Baker Eddy and his first wife were right when they said, "There is no death." In vain does Stoyte turn to Obispo to ask if there is not some point of optimum prolongation, from which the Earl's nasty life represents a decline. The heartless doctor breaks out in laughter, concluding this chain of events that has fantastically justified the absent Propter's contention that life and love, as well as good and evil, are children of time—time, that entity which betrays what it has brought into existence, and which will certainly betray those human beings who put their faith in life and love, who make absolutes of their fleeting desires.

The non-Propter sections of the novel are written with a satiric enthusiasm and a malicious inventiveness that are Huxley's natural or temperamentally spontaneous mode of artistic expression; they are in contrast with the apocalyptic, sincere, and somewhat labored Propter sections. The soda bar in Virginia's bedchamber is a symbol of the happy merging of adolescence and lust. The nuns' bodies that came with the ruins imported from Spain are *mementi mori*. Equally telling are the moat and portcullis that protect Stoyte's castle and the little shrine of the Virgin that presides over Virginia's busy bedchamber. And the ugly confrontation with eternal life in the English cellars is also done with a sure hand that deserves admiration.

Also quite admirable are passages that reflect Huxley's long concern with the tragedy of solitude—alien as such tragedy is to a thoroughly satirical presentation of experience. Jo Stoyte's refusal to meditate on death and Virginia Maitland's feeble efforts to break off with Obispo (the Virgin in her pearl-decorated shrine will understand her troubles if no one else does) are sections that carry conviction, despite the fact that their mood may be at odds with the sheer merriment of other passages.[57] But to these sections are added Propter's didacticism and apocalyptic, and these various effects do not merge successfully. But in their juxtaposition, the reader can see still more evidence of Huxley's indefatigable will, at one and the same time, to measure the inadequacies of man as he is and to sketch outlines of another figure: man as he may well become.

III   Time Must Have a Stop

The title of *Time Must Have a Stop* (1944) catches up an utterance of Shakespeare's Hotspur at the point of death: "But thought's the slave of life, and life time's fool;/And time, that takes survey of all the world,/Must have a stop." [58] These lines contain implications favorable to Huxley's view of the really complete destiny of man. When an unreflective person like Hotspur says that time must have a stop, he may mean only that human life must come to an end, and that the conquests of power and the search for sensual pleasure that animated Jo Stoyte of *After Many a Summer Dies the Swan* must halt. The reiterated thesis of Huxley's *Time Must Have a Stop* is that each man must indeed reach the last link in the chain of events that make up his life but that, for the man who has reflected and has made a wise use of his chance to exist, not everything need stop because time has run out for him.

The novel was written in the midst of the holocaust of Western civilization that Huxley, along with a great many other persons, had foreseen.[59] Uncharacteristically and in contrast with Huxley's usual habit, the main body of the novel harks back to 1929, a good many years before the period of actual composition; for many of the novels are contemporary with the year Huxley was writing them. But the Epilogue of *Time Must Have a Stop* is grimly up to date, and Huxley can function as a commentator on current events. The central figure in the novel, Sebastian Barnack, writes in his notebook, under the influence of Bruno Rontini, a Propter figure:

War guilt—the guilt of London and Hamburg, of Coventry, Rotterdam, Berlin. . . . Look at any picture paper or magazine. News . . . alternates with fiction, photographs of weapons, corpses, ruins, with photographs of half naked women. Pharisaically, I used to think there was no causal connection between these things, that, as a strict sensualist and aesthete, I was without responsibility for what was happening in the world. But the habit of sensuality and pure aestheticism is a process of God-proofing. To indulge in it is to become a spiritual mackintosh, shielding the little corner of time, of which one is the center, from the least drop of eternal reality. But the only hope for the world of time lies in being constantly drenched by that which lies beyond time.[60]

In explaining how one is to be drenched and why one should want to be, Huxley invents a rather complicated anecdote despite his contempt for mere literature and its power to strengthen the chains by which time binds man.

Time Must Have a Stop was written, moreover, about the same time that Huxley was composing his elaborately annotated collection of mystical insights, *The Perennial Philosophy* (1945), and expresses—in the meditations of two characters, Bruno Rontini and Sebastian Barnack—many of the points that were made in this treatise that goes "beyond philosophy" into the realm of insight that is true as no human, purely rational fabrication of system can be true.

As has been noted in the second chapter, Huxley's opinion is that no humanly fabricated system records much more than the genius and the limitation of some particular man, in response to the era he knew. In contrast, the "perennial philosophy" embodies insights that are true because they surpass purely human powers of thought. The "perennial philosophy," basically unchanging over the ages, is a record of what deeply intuitive men—Jesus in *some* of his sayings; the Buddha in all of his teachings; and less celebrated persons like the Germans, Tauler and Eckhart, the Spanish St. John of the Cross, and the Chinese Lao-Tze—have submitted to, have allowed themselves to be taken over by. They have allowed the self to be annihilated by a unity that includes all human egos and reduces them to homogeneity. *Time Must Have a Stop* is Huxley's most satisfactory embodiment in fiction of this "philosophy beyond philosophy."

Propter of *After Many a Summer Dies the Swan*—less well-informed than Rontini in this novel—had of course informed his audience that time would, in the natural course of events, have a stop. Rontini, however, knows precisely why it is: There is a truth superior to human truths, and men are unable to grasp it because they will to continue their immersion in the sequence of distracting event. What is borne in upon Sebastian Barnack, Bruno Rontini, and the posthumous consciousness of Sebastian's uncle, Eustace Barnack, has been anticipated in earlier novels; but it has never been so flatly stated. Moreover, in *Time Must Have a Stop* positive demonstration begins. Here is argued, both didactically and in narrative terms, the value of going beyond slavery to passion and comfort, beyond facile nihilism, beyond "goodness" even. The novel puts a representative company of modern, educated people through their paces (and the reader back in the congenial Tuscan setting of *Those Barren Leaves*) and ends with an Epilogue that writes a tendentious Q.E.D. to the earlier events. This Epilogue[61] is made up of the contact between an older and wiser Sebastian Barnack and Bruno Rontini, a relative of his who has been exhausted by Fascist cruelties. This section is more in harmony with the basic accents of the novel than are Propter's ex cathedra pronouncements in *After Many a Summer Dies the Swan*. That is, the section is a completion of what has been presented in earlier sections of the novel rather than a set of intermittent glosses.

Indeed, *Time Must Have a Stop* is, in its design and in its control of materials, the best novel Huxley wrote in his career subsequent to *Brave New World*. Particularly, in contrast to the esthetic effects observable in *After Many a Summer Dies the Swan,* the positive demonstration of what is indeed necessary for human growth is written with confidence and certainty. There are few waste motions, no explorations of blind alleys just because they are "there." *Time Must Have a Stop* is almost on a level with the three works in which Huxley, in his skeptical and "esthetic" period, achieved artistic harmony: *Crome Yellow,* an expression of the iconoclastic verve of a very young man, and *Point Counter Point* and *Brave New World,* records of a mind in the process of painful change. In contrast with these three works, *Time Must Have a Stop* expresses the certainty and conviction already noted. One must add, in all honesty, that certainty and esthetic excellence do not automatically coexist in Huxley's later work; in fact, Huxley's three remaining novels give the lie to the suggestion. But one can note that, in *Time Must Have a Stop,* certainty and a considerable degree of esthetic success do coexist.

Time Must Have a Stop has the most carefully designed plot that Huxley ever contrived. One has to be content, in reading most of the novels, with a loose concatenation of experiences—the sort of design that, as in *Point Counter Point* and *Eyeless in Gaza,* is certainly productive of ironies and intellectual comment. But, in contrast with much other work in fiction, the plot of Huxley's *Time Must Have a Stop* is made up of a sequence of events in irreversible order (hardly a remark one can make about the farce of *Antic Hay* or, for that matter, the random experiences assembled in *Point Counter Point.*)

The plot unfolds with the following sequence of events. Young Sebastian Barnack, seventeen years old and angelic in appearance, wishes to have the tokens of maturity—a dress suit and a mistress. The mistress, of course, can exist only in Sebastian's imagination; and his father refuses him the suit. John Barnack, an upper-class liberal who believes that human change is dependent on political reform, refuses to encourage his son in the cultivation of corrupt upper-class ways. (The last encounter with John Barnack in the Epilogue shows what *his* sort of hope leads to. "In some subtle and hardly explicable way" John Barnack "gave an impression of deformity—as though he had suddenly turned into a kind of dwarf or hunchback. . . . Such a man might end his life, not as a ripened human being, but as an aged foetus." [62])

After a dinner party in London that is a brilliant presentation of upper-middle-class mediocrity,[63] Sebastian travels to Florence to pay a visit to his wealthy, cultivated, and dissolute Uncle Eustace. Among the guests at the villa are three persons who count for Sebastian: Mrs. Gamble, a rich woman in her eighties, as avid for life and extension of time as Jo Stoyte—avid even though she is blind. (Of the dead, Mrs. Gamble says complacently: "They don't die. . . . They pass on." [64]) Her companion is a thirty-year-old "shameless" widow, Veronica Thwale, a more abandoned version of the type Huxley sketched in Miss Thriplow, the novelist of *Those Barren Leaves.* Mrs. Thwale, it is no surprise to learn, has been poisoned against conventional life by the virtue of her too Christian, too "good" parents. She remarks, when her host Eustace Barnack wonders why she endures employment with Mrs. Gamble: "*Your* father wasn't a poor clergyman in Islington." When she elaborates on the discomforts of a virtuous household, her litany justifies her cynicism and opportunism: "Living in a cold house.

Feeling ashamed because one's clothes are so old and shabby. But poverty wasn't the whole story. *Your* father didn't practise the Christian virtues." [65]

Mrs. Thwale takes delight—a "shameless" delight—in seducing Sebastian on the very night she has just wrung a proposal of marriage from another person who counts for Sebastian, Paul de Vries. This young American is using his fortune, made possible by a breakfast food, to advance noble causes; when he is not concerned with Mrs. Thwale, he is thinking about "the setting up of an international clearing house of ideas, the creation of a general staff of scientific-religious-philosophic synthesis for the entire planet." [66] Once more has Huxley, in these persons and others, assembled a group of persons who deceive themselves about the human lot; and perhaps Mrs. Thwale's outright sensuality is no worse than De Vries' social idealism. Both are counting on means that will destroy them; and both ignore—as do all the other persons in the novel with the exception of Sebastian in the Epilogue—the crucial and illuminating instruction of Bruno Rontini.

Sebastian's visit commences auspiciously. His Uncle Eustace approves of his nephew, likes his poetry, promises him a dress suit, and generously gives him a recently purchased Degas. But at this point everything goes wrong for Sebastian; Eustace incontinently dies in the downstairs toilet. (Eustace does not disappear from the novel at this point. For Eustace ". . . in the void and the silence there was still a kind of knowledge, a faint awareness." [67] The spoiled human awareness of Eustace hovers over the rest of the novel like a bad odor.) Sebastian, left without the promised suit, judges that he has a moral right to the Degas; the legal owner is a "good" woman, Mrs. Ockham, the stepdaughter and heir of Eustace. Sebastian sells the drawing to a Florentine dealer, and orders his suit. But Mrs. Ockham's lawyer discovers the absence of the drawing. Sebastian delays confessing what he has done, and hideous results follow his cowardice. A servant's child is badgered by the police. Much worse, Sebastian's distant relative, Bruno Rontini—a political liberal in Fascist Italy as well as a mystic—arouses the enmity of the art dealer whom he forces to give up the Degas; the dealer informs upon Bruno, who is then carried off by Fascist officers.

This tightly knit chain of events expresses, with an air of naturalness, the relations between Sebastian and his elders. The novel

is enriched or marred (judgments here must vary) by the inclu-
sion of the Epilogue, which brings Sebastian's experience up to
date (1945) and by the post-mortem experience of Uncle Eustace, which alternates with accounts of the later stages of Sebastian's youthful adventures in Florence.

The Epilogue, if it is to be defended and not just accepted as
direct preachment, serves two purposes. It gives a retrospective
view of Sebastian's later years and his continuing enslavement to
time; the high point of these years is his betrayal of his pregnant
wife by adultery with Mrs. Thwale; it seems that sexual pleasure
—an old story in Huxley's fiction—draws and repels Sebastian
with equal force. The Epilogue also recounts a meeting between
Sebastian and the persecuted Bruno Rontini. With an unwonted
generosity, Sebastian cares for Bruno until his death. Bruno's
notebook, which falls into Sebastian's willing hands, is Huxley's
concluding word on the tightly knit chain of events of past years.
Sebastian suddenly sees the meaning of all that had happened
years before in Florence. Bruno's notebooks record a special sense
of the Hotspur phrase, "Time must have a stop":

And not only *must*, as an ethical imperative and an eschatological
hope, but also *does* have a stop, in the indicative tense, as a matter
of brute experience. It is only by taking the fact of eternity into account that we can deliver thought from its slavery to life. And it is only
by deliberately paying our attention and our primary allegiance to
eternity that we can prevent time from turning our lives into a point-
less or diabolic foolery. The divine Ground is a timeless reality. Seek
it first, and all the rest . . . will be added.[68]

That significance is present for the reader, if not for Sebastian,
in other sections before the Epilogue. In these sections one observes, for example, the inconclusive battle that takes place in Eustace's continuing consciousness after his unseemly demise in the
downstairs toilet. The battle occurs between the desire of the
dead man to be free of time, sensuality, and pride of possession
and the just as strong wish (its strength owing to the unwise use
of experience in time that the living Eustace made) to return to
sensual memories, gossip, and banter. Which desire wins out in
the dead Eustace, Huxley does not indicate. But there is no doubt
that Eustace is in hell when he tries to convey, through a stupid

medium, ideas that should be useful to his friends who are still alive; the ideas come through grotesquely garbled.[69]

There is no doubt, in any case, that the defunct Eustace is a long way off from the Huxley (and, one must say at once, the Eastern) heaven in which human identity and personality are canceled and the individual consciousness is absorbed in an inclusive awareness, an indescribable nullity—two phrases that must represent man's desperate human strategies for describing that which is not human, that which is superior to the purely human labors that express themselves in historical event and produce art and literature, or science, technology and economic growth, for that matter.

One is left to fancy that the spirit of Eustace will wander for all eternity short of the experience of the infinite, bound to the trumpery displays of a second-rate medium. As Bruno Rontini had warned Eustace, the sensual man can deny himself future vision; and all that will remain for him, after death, will be the futile attempt of trying to reestablish the very bonds that condemned him to anomalous continuance. Eustace—and this tragedy is the only real one Huxley sees in human life—clings to fragments of his past self: "Ten pages of Proust, and a trot round the Bargello." Evil as these fragments seem to the persisting consciousness of Eustace, they cannot be abandoned; he had not prepared himself for the better alternative: ". . . a total self-knowledge and self-abandonment, a total attention and exposure to the light."[70] Eusace's tragedy is that time—or something like time—will not have a stop for him.

Only for Bruno—perhaps, it is suggested by materials in the Epilogue, for a Sebastian whose enlightenment is commencing—will there be an annihilation of the attachment to others, to human good and evil. Certainly no such happy fate awaits the lesser figures in the novel. Damned by their own choices to live within the confines of time are Sebastian's London relatives concerned with the collapse of their Eastern investments; Mrs. Thwale, obsessed with the seduction of young men; and De Vries, naïvely dazzled by the chance that purely political action will improve the human lot. They are no better off than poor old Mrs. Gamble, weeping for the death of her latest terrier.[71]

Of such materials and insights is *Time Must Have a Stop* composed. In this novel, human folly and servitude to time are displayed with a sure and telling wit. Folly is drawn with the skill habitual in Huxley's earlier years but not in later times. The "shamelessness" of Mrs. Thwale as she initiated her seduction of Sebastian during the séance,[72] the heartlessness of Eustace as he puts off a visit to an old mistress in order to enjoy a perverse afternoon with a more recent one,[73] the groundless fantasies of the young Sebastian—all are done with memorable skill. Moreover, in much of the novel there is an element of drama, of real contest and tension among the imperfect, unenlightened wills of the chief characters. But it must be confessed that drama evaporates from the Epilogue. The reasons for this one can suspect; Sebastian and Bruno now move in an ambience hostile to drama of any sort: the ambience of full illumination. Here is an ambience indifferent to—if not hostile to—drama of any sort. Still later novels manifest more deeply than this one the marks of flaccidity that announce the presence of a certain kind of religious illumination.

IV Ape and Essence

As previously noted, there is always a strong element of the contemporaneous in the novels of Huxley. This element will eventually date them, though it does not do so as yet, perhaps because the particular stimuli to which Huxley reacted are still vivid parts of our view of the present and of the recent past that has formed the present. At any rate, in the novels just considered in this chapter there is certainly a keen sense of the newspaper headlines of the time: the rise of the great totalitarianisms of the 1930's and their fruition in war, and the apparent powerlessness of democratic nationalism to be an effective counter-irritant to these threats to individual and collective human dignity. If interest in Huxley's novels survives into another century, there will certainly be need for explanations of Huxley's references to the fall of Barcelona in *After Many a Summer Dies the Swan* and to the death of Gandhi spoken of in the opening pages of *Ape and Essence*.[74] For a man who was moving to an intellectual position that encouraged contempt for what occurred in time, Huxley's imagination is startlingly linked to current event.

Ape and Essence records once more Huxley's repugnance to uncritical faith in progress, the dangerous worship in parts of the world of the totalitarian vision and in others of the just-as-dangerous blend of democracy and nationalism that Huxley could be keenly aware of in England and in southern California. This was the general situation of his time. But particular events, particular headlines, are always putting thumbscrews on Huxley's imagination. A further stage of civilization's collapse is what Huxley found in the events that concluded World War II; such events in fact led him to speak confidently of World War III in *Ape and Essence*.[75] The explosion of the atom bomb ("The Thing," as it is referred to in *Ape and Essence*) is but a prelude to a reign of destructive violence that will plunge mankind backward into decades of waste and loss. The murder of Gandhi, spoken of in the prologue of *Ape and Essence,* is but a sign that the only way out of twentieth-century troubles—the way of a pacifism and non-violence that leads to vision—is not going to be followed.

Ape and Essence is what one might call a "black" utopia; and it is not, like *Brave New World,* an ironic projection of the optimism about the future that kindles in the popular mind—a projection that asked men whether this future world was what they actually wanted. *Ape and Essence* is, instead, a promise of what men are very shortly actually going to experience. Instead of the age of "our Ford" will come that of Belial, the father of lies, the author of evil, who will be the reigning principle. Mankind must realize that it is on the verge of a period when the human hand will make not the sign of the Model T but the sign of the horns which are Belial's conventional symbol: horns that express animality, mindlessness, regression.

Huxley's presentation of the kingdom of Belial rises often to a frantic if somewhat unconvincing shriek. One must grant that, in comparison with *Nineteen Eighty-four,* Orwell's "black" utopia, *Ape and Essence* is hasty and superficial. But the book has, nevertheless, deep interest since repugnances and convictions less clear elsewhere in Huxley come to the surface in it. Hatreds of sexuality and conventional religion have unbridled expression. Fear, horror, concern—about these matters and others—blossom in the novel as swiftly as the atomic cloud itself.

The novel begins with a somewhat gratuitous prologue in present-day Hollywood and its environs. When two studio executives come across a script written by one William Tallis, they journey into the California desert to interview the author. But Tallis is dead, buried under a Joshua tree (which, neatly, the fleeing lovers of Tallis' script come across on the last page of the dead man's work). The visiting executives learn something about Tallis, the eccentric solitary who had set down his vision of evil times to come. Tallis, the visitors are told, had been moved beyond measure by the horrors of the World War II, by the likelihood (for example) that an unknown German granddaughter of his had had to sell her body to survive. Yet the affronts to human personality in such a transaction—the visitors guess—were hardly less shocking to Tallis than "saturation bombing" and the atomic explosion itself.

Huxley's tendency to hit every target in sight is classically illustrated in this prologue. One of the intellectual Hollywood visitors offers insincere encouragement to a young woman with cinematic ambitions: an instance, once more, of the "high brows, low loins" which Rampion of *Point Counter Point* censured in Spandrell.[76] The other visitor is disgusted by the presence of a nursing child and its diapers. Neither detail contributes anything to the relation between the prologue and the scenario which tells of the future.

After this not particularly illuminating delay, the curtain finally rises on the bleak future. The events are presented in the rather stiff form of a motion picture script, where there are often indications as to how a scene is to be played and photographed. (Huxley had himself done work of this sort for Hollywood.) Dialogue is set down, actions are described, and there are frequent indications of the voice of a narrator who plainly is speaking for the agonized Tallis and for the no less suffering Huxley. The most one can say for the device is that it obviates the need for a Propter figure.

As the script begins, the reader finds himself in southern California, amid the ruins of museums, universities, industrial units, and highways that once linked them into a kind of civilization—one that Huxley cast saturnine glances at in *After Many a Summer Dies the Swan*. Among these ruins lives a scattering of human beings who are hanging on to what is left of civilization. Their genetic endowment has been distorted by radiation from "The Thing" (the atom bomb). Loola, the heroine, is fairly normal, except for an extra pair of nipples. Had she been born with more than fourteen fingers, for example, she would have been slaughtered at a religious festival. Human mastery over nature is almost gone; and crews of helots are sent to dig up the Hollywood cemetery (apparently the same one that, in all its glory, exists in *After Many a Summer Dies the Swan*) for the rings, bracelets, and clothes that man can no longer manufacture. These helots—a word that Huxley does not use but one that is proper for describing the condition of Loola and her male and female peers—live without sexual relations except for the two weeks in the year that are set aside for breeding purposes. Loola's simple garment has the word *no* stitched over her breasts and her buttocks; the garments that bear these prohibitions are appropriately torn off during the Saturnalia sanctioned by the god Belial and his priesthood.

The society is, in fact, a monstrous theocracy, directed by the eunuchs who make up the priestly caste. These men wear headdresses adorned with Satanic horns and deliver sermons that celebrate the triumph of their destructive deity. The society—as the priests often observe with venomous regret—has its deviants: the Hots, who are moved by sexual desire throughout the year. These persons, moreover, resemble a deviant like Bernard Marx in *Brave New World;* they wish to form individual attachments marked by personal as well as sexual concern. Their concern is aroused not by the reading of Shakespeare—as in *Brave New World* where, as here, everyone belongs to everyone else—but of Shelley, whose passages express the need for spiritual affinity between human beings.[77] Hots, it may be noted, are buried alive if they are detected. If they are prudent, they try to escape to a reservation of Hots somewhere north of Fresno.

Into this society of helots comes a band of scientists from New Zealand, which has not been touched by "The Thing." The priesthood quickly liquidates the visitors who, by their rationality, are threats to the rule of Belial. Only one man—a biologist named Poole—is allowed to survive because he can provide plans for augmenting the dwindling food supply in California. Poole is—it should not surprise the reader of Huxley—subject to a prudery which veils an incestuous dependence on his mother in New Zealand. Perhaps in the interest of advancing the plot of *Ape and Essence,* Poole overcomes his inhibitions at the time of the Saturnalia and has intercourse with the willing Loola. But he wishes after the licit time to continue the relationship, as does Loola herself; they are Hots. When Poole is quickly invited to become a eunuch, he and Loola flee northward to Fresno, passing on their hegira the Joshua tree near the tomb of the predictive Tallis, the author of their adventure.

Such is the narrative substance of the next to the last of Huxley's utopian visions. (The last utopia, *Island*, is not "black"; instead, it harks back to the optimism of Bellamy's *Looking Backward* and H. G. Wells' *Men Like Gods*.) If one follows out the implied contrast in the title—*Ape and Essence*—one has an indication of the point of Tallis' scenario: a vision of a mankind that has abandoned its essence—rationality and spirituality—and has sunk into a worse-than-anthropoid condition. It is worse because the behavior of an ape represents faithfulness to simian capacities; whereas the bestiality of the two-week saturnalia subtracts from human beings what, in other ages, they occasionally enjoyed. Sheerly impossible for Loola and her kind is any refinement by reason of instinctive behavior and, for a happy few, the passage beyond reason to modes of being that unite man and the ground of all existence. This second sort of "essence" is not even dreamed of by poor bestialized Loola as she laboriously struggles toward the relative good of being a person, an individual.

Occasionally, the voice on the scenario soundtrack mentions what is not present—the noble opportunities that Belial and his priests make sure will not open to Loola and her kind. Sadly, Poole assures Loola that there is indeed something stronger than Belial and that Belial cannot finally win: "Because He can never resist the temptation of carrying evil to the limit. And whenever evil is carried to the limit, it always destroys itself. After which the Order of Things comes to the surface again." Loola replies: "But .that's far away in the future." Poole answers: "For the whole world, yes. But not for the single individual, not for you or me, for example. Whatever Belial may have done with the rest of the world, you and I can always work with the Order of Things not against it." [78] But, as matters stand in the world of *Ape and Essence*, the potentiality in each person is gravely inhibited. As has been noted, it is inhibited in *Brave New World* by the excess of dependence on comfort and distraction; but it is inhibited in *Ape and Essence* by the outright slavery and the abuse of power. What chance have most of Loola's peers for the "self-validating experience" [79] which gives Poole courage to think of escaping? Very little.

Indeed, faced by the dangers of the realm of Belial, where is

one to flee? The Savage in *Brave New World* had only the primi-
tive, instinctual life to flee to; but Poole and Loola do well when
they turn away from the very life of instinct. Huxley, with some
acuteness, makes no attempt to saddle Poole and Loola with the
"high arguments" known to Bruno Rontini in *Time Must Have a
Stop*. The most that Poole and Loola will achieve, if they ever get
to Fresno and the benevolent Hots there, is an esteem for each
other's limited personality. Poole and Loola will do well if they
are simply able to be human; emancipating vision will be out of
the question.

That the realm of Belial is essentially one of rampant sexuality
is emphasized by the descriptions of the two weeks of license. The
yearly Saturnalia is described in ways that underline the confusions potential in all sexual experience: "Silhouettes of men pursuing women, or women throwing themselves on men, appear for a
moment and vanish. To the accompaniment of the Good Friday
music we hear a rising and falling chorus of grunts and moans, of
explosively shouted obscenities and long-drawn howls of agoniz-
ing delight." Huxley's comments make clear that this priestly manipulation of sexuality is not healthy animal expression but a
ghastly retreat from the combination of instinct and rationality
that can at times mark human copulation: "Thanks to the su-
preme Triumph of Modern Science, sex has become seasonal,
romance has been swallowed up by the oestrus and the female's
chemical compulsion to mate has abolished courtship, chivalry,
tenderness, love itself." [80] There is—and here the matter must rest
—an unresolved ambiguity in Huxley's depiction of sex. Only a
prudery of a deep and temperamental sort can explain Huxley's
all-too-frequent depiction of heroes who embrace their mistresses
with a sense of disgust for what they are doing.

V   The Genius and the Goddess

The Genius and the Goddess (1955) is Huxley's last attempt to
express in something like dramatic terms his view of human action
and its sources. More clearly than anywhere else are the difficulties of using the vistas of "clear light" (a phrase for the benefits of
vision used recurrently in *Island*, the last work of fiction)[81] as
illumination for the stage of human action. The difficulties of putting Eastern religious insight to such use are much greater than
those faced by a novelist who has gone beyond the limits of Natu-

ralism or Humanist insight in his effort to present man's experience in a Christian vista. Christian vistas allow continued attention to the particularity and the individuality of the persons being
presented. It is true that the Christian novelist—Dostoyevsky or
Bernanos—imports into his novel resolutions of human problems
that are inadmissible in work that centers attention on man and
man alone. But, even so, the novels of Dostoyevsky and Bernanos
keep attention fixed on particular suffering human beings even
though these two novelists read that suffering as a loss, a depriva-
tion, of the presence of a deity at once personal and yet transcendent. In their novels, human individuality—enriched, some
would say; diminished, others would assert—still occupies the attention.

Huxley faces a quite different problem, as *The Genius and the
Goddess* in its minor way suggests. Human personality itself, as
Huxley makes quite clear in his theoretical speculation,[82] is—like
the fall of primordial unity into the diversity that initiated the
world as man knows it—a lamentable deviation into particularity.
The "fall" in each man is the continuation of that greater "fall"
which took place when the divine principle—the "Clear Light,"
the nullity—permitted itself to be partitioned out in what one
may call "the works of creation." The corrective to man's "fallen"
condition, his sense of apartness, is quite unlike Christian "grace,"
which aids man without effecting a cancellation of his identity.
Huxleyan "grace" is a corrective that reveals the unity that underlies the diversity so deceptive to all men.

The result of such "grace" is a vision that nullifies—as Christian
"grace" does not—any deep curiosity about the shape of one's
own personality and its special destiny. Such a nullification, it
would seem, would be disenabling to a novelist whose stock in
trade is separate human beings and their bewildering interplay
with one another. *The Genius and the Goddess* is more than an
incidental testimony to the limitations that Huxley's mature convictions about man put on his work as a novelist.

In works where Huxley seems to feel quite free to manipulate
events (*After Many a Summer Dies the Swan, Ape and Essence*),
the restrictive quality of his view of man does not appear in its
entire force. With some effectiveness, *Time Must Have a Stop*
makes the point that time must not be worshipped as the decisive
mark of man's experience and that a fixed personality must not be

cherished as the chief mark of being human. True, man must not be reduced to less than human: a point made with a rather heavy hand in *Ape and Essence*. But "being human" is, after all, a second-rate kind of excellence. The merit of "being human" is chiefly that it opens the way to the last journey of all: the journey to being more than human, the journey that takes man beyond time and human individuality.

On its surface, *The Genius and the Goddess* has the air of limiting attention to the individual and to the special problems of three or four persons—problems that are different from the representative or typical dilemmas faced by a person like Jo Stoyte in *After Many a Summer Dies the Swan.* A summary of the events in *The Genius and the Goddess* suggests that the reader is in the presence of some sort of psychological realism. An actual reading of the novel points to other conclusions: the work is close to other Huxley fiction that, in surface structure and subject-matter, it does not resemble.

The use of John Rivers, the American narrator and protagonist, keeps the problem of the central intelligence or awareness in order. Rivers, a very old man when he confides his recollections to a friend, belongs to Huxley's own generation and thus can draw on a range of reference that one would grant an American counterpart of Huxley's earlier British heroes. (There are modish references to Thurber, Mickey Spillane, and the war in Korea;[83] but the intellectual climate is otherwise that of a good many years earlier.)

In this tale that seems to give promise of an unwonted psychological realism one notes that the American teller has his full complement of Huxley's incidental prejudices. John Rivers wonders if one can think of any of Henry James' characters using the bathroom.[84] He sees that each person's "intrinsically golden" opportunity to experience for himself is destroyed by the accepted ideas of a particular time and place: ". . . of course if you're sufficiently steeped in the tripe and hogwash dished out by the molders of public opinion, you'll tend automatically to pollute your impressions at the source; you'll recreate the world in the image of your own notions—and of course your own notions are everybody else's notions. . . ."[85]

Rivers, moreover, has a past that is an American transposition of the pasts of Anthony Beavis in *Eyeless in Gaza* and other heroes. For Rivers has been dominated by a mother whose Lutheran piety kept her son a virgin until the age of twenty-eight. And Huxley, as usual, sees this maternal domination as incestuous at its basis and as disastrous in its consequences. Rivers says to the auditor of his tale: "My poor mother . . . I suppose I could have been kinder to her. But however kind I might have been, it wouldn't have altered the fundamental facts—the fact that she loved me possessively, and the fact that I didn't want to be possessed . . . ; the fact that she was a proud Stoic, living in the illusion that she was a Christian, and the fact that I had lapsed into a wholesome paganism. . . ." [86] It is an old story in Huxley; the love of a "good" mother—a love centered on the person of a child—can erect barriers to that child's mastery of his highest destiny, which is the cancellation of himself as a being who takes any kind of human love very seriously.

Early in the novel, Rivers recollects *his* growth in grace, his movement beyond the restrictive moral and emotional framework which hedges in most people. (It is an arrested growth, by Huxley's standards.) Rivers tells how, as a young physicist, he became a member of the household of a "genius," the great physicist Henry Maartens. He is a monument of intellectual power whose hypertrophe in one direction makes him grotesquely dependent on the radiant physical presence of his "goddess" wife, Kathy. The relation between the emotionally sterile Maartens and Kathy recalls two of the husband-wife relations in the early *Point Counter Point*. Quarles must have the aid of his wife Eleanor if he is to establish any relations at all with his world; she is his "majordomo." The powerful but impractical Rampion needs the support of the social confidence and the animal wisdom of his wife, Mary. As with Quarles and Rampion, Maartens is dependent on the "leadings" that his superb wife provides.

The young Rivers was happy in this potentially explosive household. But the old Rivers, as he recollects, devotes what seems to the reader an inordinate space to his youthful attention to the intellectual growth of Ruth, the daughter of the family. Presently Ruth is dropped as an object of interest, and the young Rivers becomes involved in the relation between the dependent husband and the radiant wife. Kathy has to go to Chicago to tend her dying mother; Maartens promptly becomes ill, as he has during Kathy's previous absences. It is clear that Kathy must return if he is to be saved. She does so; but she is depleted in strength and has nothing to offer her husband.

On the very night of her return, she enters—in apparent desperation—the room where Rivers is sleeping, overcomes his not very formidable Lutheran resistance, and from the night of love with the young man renews the radiance that her husband needs. Kathy manages the young Rivers firmly, and an Olympian transcendence of ordinary moral scruple sets in. Here, in part, are Rivers' later meditations on his loss of virginity in a noble cause. Kathy

was a kind of feminine Antaeus—invincible while her feet were in the ground, a goddess so long as she was in contact with the greater goddess within her, the universal Mother without. Three weeks of attendance on a dying woman had broken that contact. Grace came when it was restored. . . . An hour of love, five or six hours of the deep otherness of sleep, and the emptiness was filled, the ghost reincarnated. She lived again—yet not she, of course, but the Unknown Quantity lived in her. . . . At one end of the spectrum it's pure spirit, it's the Clear Light of the Void; and at the other end it's instinct, it's health, it's the perfect functioning of an organism that's infallible so long as we don't interfere with it; and somewhere between the two extremes is what St. Paul called "Christ"—the divine made human. Spiritual grace, animal grace, human grace—these aspects of the same underlying mystery, ideally, all of us should be open to all of them.[87]

This passage, like many others in Huxley's later work, bears witness to his transformation of familiar religious terms; "ghost," "grace," and "spirit" troop by but are to be understood only in the often novel contexts Huxley provides for them. Particularly significant is the triple phrase—"spiritual grace, animal grace, human grace." Their relation to one another and to man's final, inclusive destiny is the prime topic of Huxley's last novel, *Island.*

The vivifying happiness that the relation between Rivers and Kathy makes possible is quickly destroyed by Ruth, who is deeply jealous of her mother. During a quarrel, both Kathy and Ruth die in an auto wreck. The dependent husband—and here lies heavy irony—is *not* destroyed by the loss of his goddess but goes on to two other marriages; as an "overwound clockwork monkey," Maartens goes on to work on the atom bomb and to spin out "gaily apocalyptic speculations about the bigger and better Infernal Machines of the future." [88]

The Genius and the Goddess is a tighter, more controlled work than any of the other novels considered in this chapter, with the possible exception of the non-visionary sections of *Time Must Have a Stop*. But in reading the actual novel, one experiences a narrative texture in which there are a minimum of depiction of what happens (the bedchamber encounter is indeed presented more fully and more sympathetically than any other such scene) and a maximum of meditation on the meaning of the story told. This meditation upon event—unlike that of Marlowe in *Lord Jim* or of James' many commentators or "reflectors"—turns one *away* from the story being told rather than drives one into a consideration of the deep complexities of a certain person's motives.

First, one can say that the meditation ceases to be that of an elderly American named Rivers; it becomes transparently that of an elderly English writer who threads the Rivers speculations with references and wit which are hardly what one would expect of a physicist, but which are, indeed, just what one has come to expect of English writer Huxley. (When Rivers speaks of Maartens' early and, at that time, baseless suspicions of his wife, the word that describes the physicist's baseness is "dung-slide"; it is nothing less than a "sub-human soliloquy." [89] This, in its context, is an intemperate use of language for shock-purposes that is much more common in Huxley than the present analysis has suggested.) And, though Rivers' nose is kept fairly close to the narrative grindstone, he is allowed to come to conclusions about the genius and his goddess that make the entire story less a narrative concerned with the crucial involvement of persons than one more fable illustrative of a section of Huxley's mature convictions.

And this point deserves underlining. Rivers explains his own early years as those of a boy who was immersed in moral distinctions that, in the long run, simply do not count—that are wisely forgotten in the arms of a goddess who is seeking revival of her powers. And the character of the "genius"—a being whose merit must be taken for granted since, in the pages of the novel, one hears of his attacks of asthma and little else—is just one more depiction of the sin of intellectual isolation: a sin, for Huxley, hardly less heinous than the moralism that binds Rivers.

Finally, almost as if in a masque or a tableau, Kathy is the force of instinctive life itself. She is hardly knowable as a person and has to be understood as an embodiment of wisdom—wisdom at least when the health of her being is compared to the illnesses of the two men. But Huxley makes clear that one is not to conclude that Kathy exists as a late and pious salute to the teachings of D. H. Lawrence. Kathy is "right"; but she is not so "right" as she might be. Unlike her moralist lover and her aridly intellectual husband, she is fully the creature of sense that every human being ought to be. She does not, however, "go on" from this good condition to become fully the creature of spirit that, in Huxley's judgment, each human being also has the chance to become.

One need not quarrel with Huxley's possession of mature convictions; many great novelists have had them. But one has a right to observe that, once more, Huxley's cluster of beliefs about man render him inattentive to the human beings he has chosen to create. One must also note that none of the three main personages of *The Genius and the Goddess* goes "beyond" conventional experience, as Sebastian Barnack in *Time Must Have a Stop* is prepared to do and as the hero in *Island* actually does. Because they do not achieve high goals of illumination, they do not deeply attract the interest of their creator. What they are is either the just object of satirical attention (the sexual purity of the teller and the intellectual complacency of the physicist are laughable) or regret—the wife, alas, falls short of being the whole creature she had a chance to be.

That Huxley's limitations in serious characterization—in this novel and elsewhere—are consequent upon limitation of his own literary temperament is a fact impossible to deny; ceaseless in Huxley is the drive to draw a picture of human motives that reveals insincerity and pretension, as in Ruth, the daughter, in this novel. But it is a drive that finds further warrant in Huxley's developed view of man: man is, at his best, the being who can cease to be man—the being whose most significant gesture effects a break, a discontinuity, between all that he has been and what he may become. The result of this central conviction is a habitual indifference to the essence of each person. All of Huxley's characters are in danger of becoming schematic lay figures that resemble one another or, at least, identical figures in other novels. Huxley writes a kind of modern *commedia dell' arte*, with Columbine and Harlequin bearing different names from novel to novel but actually being dominated by their set roles, their set utterances, and their set tragedies.

CHAPTER 6

Two Biographies

SEPARATED by eleven years—*Grey Eminence* appeared in 1941 and *The Devils of Loudun* in 1952—are two works of Huxley's that are in a class by themselves, or appear to be at first inspection. Unlike the novels, they are accounts of events that actually happened rather than calculated manipulations of Huxley's own experience of his era. Unlike the utopias, *Brave New World* and *Ape and Essence,* they represent an attempt to read aright sections of the real past rather than to arouse shudders in the presence of an imagined future. And unlike many of the essays, the two biographies represent a prolonged and careful discipline of study rather than brilliant insight stimulated by a leafing through of Goya's *Desastres de la Guerra,* a contemplation of the Breughels in Vienna, or a visit to Sabbioneta,[1] a planned town in Italy.

This contrast offered by *Grey Eminence* and *The Devils of Loudun* is real. They are studies of seventeenth-century French religion and politics. By length at least they are even set apart from other instructive studies of sections of the past, like the essays on the religious charlatan, the Reverend Henry James Prince; on the French philosopher, Maine de Biran; on the Italian composer Gesualdo; and on the twentieth-century American Socialist, Job Harriman.[2] But like these shorter studies, the two biographies manifest an attitude toward the past that one should expect of Huxley. The past, for him, does not so much exist as an object worthy of study in its own right but is an opportunity to recognize some moral or esthetic disease or disorder that works unrecognized in some section of the present. He continues, in these long books, the sort of inspection that one encounters in an early essay like "Comfort,"[3] in which the study of the Renaissance taste for space and grandeur allows a more just estimate of the modern taste for coziness. The art of such an essay lies in taking up a subject, establishing a contrast that creates a startling but justifiable *aperçu*, and then quickly concluding. In *Grey Eminence* and *The Devils of Loudun,* Huxley does not conclude.

Instead, Huxley pushes in these two books his investigation of a selected section of the past to some length. He sustains his dogged analysis of the meaning of two segments of seventeenth-century experience as, of course, he has no need to do in an essay like the one on the seventeenth-century Italian composer Gesualdo. But in the two heroes of the biographies he finds just the sort of oddity that challenged him more briefly in the experience of Gesualdo, a man whose passional and religious experience contained the sort of quaint abnormality to which Huxley's attention veers as readily as a weathercock in a sudden breeze. Gesualdo killed his faithless wife and her lover; and, in a picture that his late-blooming piety caused to be painted, he had himself represented as rising to the heavenly embrace of Christ while his dead wife and her paramour endured the torments of hell in a lower corner of the picture.[4] This piquant detail is not alien in its preposterousness to the deformations of the religious experience which drew Huxley to Père Urbain Grandier, the hero of *The Devils of Loudun,* and to Père Joseph du Tremblay, the subject of *Grey Eminence.*

Yet, contrasts admitted, striking relations between these two books and Huxley's other work exist. As a biographer, he remembers and uses skills he acquired as a novelist and an essayist. He is an historian who, more often than most professional historians, suspends the onward march of event to compose paragraphs and even chapters of discursive analysis of the meaning, the sheer human sense or nonsense, of the events that he has just been relating.[5] He exercises, in such passages, the essayist's prerogative to intersperse a narrative with circling elaborations that alter the shape of an event from what it apparently was to what it is or may be. And it is a novelist's prerogative to go beyond explicit evidence and to fill it out as the source materials do not—all with the intent of giving the richness of folly, misery, and acutest suffering not supplied by crumbling documents.

An analysis of the two books quickly indicates that Huxley goes beyond the work of sober historical reconstruction which, at many points, they do indeed contain. On his work of reconstruction Huxley erects a thesis. Perceptions are not followed up simply because they have come to an author rich in ingenuity; they are

explored as part of the unfolding of the chosen thesis. The grotesque ceases to be esteemed for its own amusing sake. (Such
soberness is not habitual with Huxley. One recalls that no tears
are shed for the idiotic Miss Elver in *Those Barren Leaves* and
that only an amused stare is offered the victims of a nineteenth
century religious imposter in the essay entitled "Justifications." [6])
In the two biographies, Huxley's pleasure in dazzling himself and
others with the lightning of his own perceptions is in abeyance.
Rather do both biographies participate in the elaboration of
theses that dominate Huxley's mind from the mid-1930's onward
—theses that receive a more general treatment in *Ends and
Means, The Perennial Philosophy,* and other books.

It is with *The Perennial Philosophy* that the two biographies
are most closely linked. As noted in the second chapter of this
study, *The Perennial Philosophy*—useful also for understanding
Time Must Have a Stop and other later novels—is an exposition
of the synthesis Huxley has made from his mental travels in many
directions: in the regions of science, esthetics, and literature, and
in the widespread terrain of mystical experience. The two biographies mine the past to demonstrate the soundness of the convictions arrived at in *The Perennial Philosophy.*

The convictions, briefly, are these. The redemption of man rests
not on ritual observance or orthodoxy, not on conscious pursuit of
suffering in an imitation of a savior named Jesus. Instead, redemption comes from a radical reorientation of human awareness
that renders a future kingdom of heaven unnecessary and dogmas
about a transcendent deity an irrelevance. The reorientation also
transforms one's estimate of whatever has seemed important in
"the world"; much that has seemed important—politics, physical
pleasure, or knowledge *per se*—moves to the periphery of attention or beyond it. For at the center of attention lies an incom-
municable awareness of a new relationship to a principle of unity
that binds together all experience. This awareness, rather than the
death of a divine-human savior on a cross, redeems distressed and
distracted men.

Huxley, in illustration of this crucial point, remarks of the inacceptable mysticism of Bérulle, a seventeenth-century teacher of
the arts of religious meditation: "Bérulle no doubt sincerely be-
lieved that the soul could adhere to the Incarnate Word or to the
Virgin in exactly the same way as it could adhere to God, and

with the same consequences. But, psychologically, this is impossible. There cannot be adherence to persons or personal qualities without analysis and imagination; and where analysis and imagination are active, the mind is unable to receive into itself the being of God." [7]

Bérulle and all religious teachers who try to center the deepest mystical experience on a suffering savior or a weeping Mother are setting up a discipline of an inferior order. The most Huxley will concede of such a path is that "It was a path that would lead them [the pupils] to virtue. . . . It was also a path that would lead them to intense, affective devotion to divine persons, and to untiring activity on their behalf. But it was not a path that would lead to union with ultimate reality." [8] Ultimate reality, as Huxley has learned to think of it—learned chiefly from Eastern instructors—lies beyond the personality of any nameable being, no matter how august.

Both *Grey Eminence* and *The Devils of Loudun* are negative demonstrations of this truth. Both books—implicitly in the tales which Huxley resurrects from the past and explicitly in the full commentary he provides—show the cost in misery and the sadness of neglected possibilities that come from faulty estimates of man's position. *Grey Eminence* is the more thoroughgoing demonstration; it concerns a protagonist who has the truth in his grasp (or nearly) and thinks that he can go on reaching for other things —power in particular. In contrast, *The Devils of Loudun* is chiefly concerned with persons who have little inkling that they have missed their chance to live fully, to achieve a relation with unity that underlies diverse, discontinuous human experience. For Huxley, of course, this unity is a deity without face or form and cannot flatter man's interest in his individual existence. Like the Divine of the fourteenth-century German mystics, or the Principle venerated by the Gnostics, or the nullity at the heart of much Hindu and Buddhist spirituality, Huxley's One is without face or form, or qualities of any kind.

I   The Devils of Loudun

The dramatis personae of the two books overlap. The hero of the second book, the rash and worldly Père Urbain Grandier of *The Devils of Loudun,* has the misfortune to add to his local troubles the antipathy of Richelieu and Richelieu's "grey eminence,"

Père Joseph.[9] A more important overlapping than this one is the fact that the two books share a background: France in the first half of the seventeenth century, recovering from the civil warfare of the previous century.

This warfare was in part occasioned by the confusions created in France and elsewhere by the Protestant Reformation and the Catholic Counter Reformation. Added to this change was the difficulty caused in France by disputes about the royal succession. Under Richelieu, power was being centered in the throne, at the expense of the nobles; the king of France and his ministers needed this power to challenge the Austrian and Spanish forces that surrounded them. In particular, the international problems that created and protracted the Thirty Years' War in Germany bulk large in *Grey Eminence;* these demanded the attention of Richelieu and his aide, the Capuchin monk Joseph du Tremblay. Less concerned with these inclusive matters is *The Devils of Loudun;* at the fore in this book are the perverted religious sensibilities of the time.

But both books, whatever their contrasts in range, drive toward the main point which is Huxley's concern: the mystery of man's rejection of his great opportunity—the chance to be aware of the divine unity, and to unite himself with that unity by prayer and meditation. Both books are tragedies if, indeed, it be a tragedy to fail to be a saint. Huxley's estimate of what it is to be a saint differs from the traditional Catholic one, as he points out especially in *Grey Eminence.* The conventional Catholic saint of recent centuries turns toward the specific figures of the Christian pantheon—particularly toward Jesus and Mary. These figures, revere them as one may, are barriers to the "Clear Light" that shines for the mystic who is free—as some Catholic mystics are not—of devotion to adored, specific figures and of dogmas with which orthodox mystical experience has to be aligned.

Huxley remarks that an older group of Christian mystics—those who followed Dionysian traditions—"had adapted dogma to their own experience, with the result that, in so far as they were advanced mystics, they had ceased to be specifically Catholic." The possession of such liberty is crucial for the mystic; to see the importance of this freedom is to grasp what Huxley has in mind whenever he speaks of spiritual fulfillment and ultimate reality. Only such freedom "provides the basis for a religion free from unacceptable dogmas, which themselves are contingent upon ill established and arbitrarily interpreted historical facts." [10]

This important passage—important for understanding the concern that animates much of Huxley's later work—casts light on Huxley's recurring impatience with Christianity long after he has ceased to be cavalier toward religion in general. The truly wise person is—must be—that person who moves beyond his devotion to Jesus and Mary. Instead, he seeks a relation with the immanent unity that informs every nook and cranny of the universe; this latter principle is simply waiting to be known, to be united with, by the man or woman who achieves a transformation of his own awareness.

Serving this insight, Huxley fashions two cautionary tales. The essential point of these tales is not different from that advanced in *Time Must Have a Stop* (1944), where the man who dies, Eustace Barnack, experiences the tragedy of being earthbound, of realizing that his sensuality has inhibited insights that go beyond the raptures provided by a pretty Florentine woman. Grandier's failure in *The Devils of Loudun* is that of a man who, despite his priestly calling, was hardly aware of the opportunities he was bypassing. Père Joseph's failure is, as Huxley reads it, more moving and horrifying. For Père Joseph was, as a young man, a person who had felt a call to the spiritual life; whereas Grandier, handsome and talented and yet relatively obscure, had regarded the church as a stage where his talents could be displayed and as an avenue which often led to the bedchambers of lovely penitents.

The Devils of Loudun, then, is primarily a brilliant study in what might be called religious morbid psychology—morbid because the book is concerned with a great many persons who misunderstand the opportunities that various religious vocations offer them. There is the morbidity of Grandier, who easily dismissed from his mind the implications of the religion he served—dismissed them until it was almost too late, until he was broken on the rack and tied to the metal seat where he would be burned to death. The perversion of Grandier is horrifying enough, but not really a strain on the reader's powers of understanding. The history of religion is full of persons who answer the call of Christ as if it summoned one to a profession little more demanding than the iron-mongery and the contract-writing of the men of Loudun who were Grandier's enemies.

The real depths of perversity, of religion gone awry, are reached by the Ursuline nuns who, following the example of their unworthy prioress, Jeanne des Anges, court demonic possession. This occult invasion of foreign wills—so the hysterical nuns believe—has its immediate origin in Grandier's evil power. The nuns are convinced that this disturbance comes ultimately from Satan himself and not, as one might say today, from levels of the unconscious. With a relish that the reader must recognize, Huxley describes the contortions that the poor ladies undergo. With a relentless attention (not new to the readers of his fiction) Huxley traces the effects of the frustrated sexuality and religious ignorance that keep the convent in an uproar and transform it into an equivalent of the sword-swallower's booth at a fair.

But Huxley's contempt for the nuns and for Grandier is more qualified than it is in early novels where, for example, the self-deception of the "Franciscan" Burlap, in *Point Counter Point*, wins nothing but laughter because it is so obviously beyond the pale of common sense. The hysteria of the nuns and the complacent pursuit of sensuality and power on the priest's part are *not* beyond the pale. Instead, the failure of Mère Jeanne des Anges and the self-deception of the handsome priest are representative of the failures that men in all centuries encounter. The nuns and the priest are immersed in folly—true. And it is folly that leads to the grotesque inconsequence of the events at Loudun—to the hysteria-induced signs of special divine favor on the hand of the Prioress (the names of Jesus, Mary, St. Joseph, and St. François de Sales appeared there and were widely exhibited by the Prioress in her travels) and to the graver waste of priestly talent. But it is not folly that can be regarded as incomprehensible, as is much of the invented folly in the Huxley novels of the 1920's. In those novels, analogous folly is just *there*, to amuse the author and his intelligent readers. The folly of *The Devils of Loudun* is, in contrast, one that illuminates the pattern of folly in modern man's own experience, though he is possessed not by devils but by more reputable causes of alienation from his proper destiny. If the reader finds Grandier's misreading of his own purposes comically stupid, what of his own?

The Devils of Loudun is Huxley's most moving book. Despite the long, essay-like sections on satanic possession and the general uncertainty man has about his purposes,[11] Huxley's account of the priest and the insane nuns moves with authority. It escapes the defects of the novels, the chief of which are random improvisation of event, and comment on event that is forced and often (for the perceptive reader) gratuitous. There is, in *The Devils of Loudun*, nothing gratuitous or forced in the chapters which tell of the appalling mental disorders that overtake the poor sisters, the exorcists who come to drive out demons and establish their own clerical reputations, and the mass of townsmen and visitors who find the writhing sisters an enchanting but horrifying spectable. The history of the poor, contemptible Urbain Grandier moves toward the rack and the stake with an inevitability that is lacking from Huxley's accounts of human action that he, rather than life and past history, invented.

The powerful effect of this book and of the scarcely less powerful *Grey Eminence* depends not only on life and past history but on Huxley's acute perception as he looks carefully into the documents and secondary sources he works from and adds to them believable explanations (for example, his analysis of the probable motives of the exorcists, who are charmed by the opportunity to please God by exercising absolute power over the nuns[12]). It is an artistic achievement of the first order to be able to reconstitute such a person as Grandier—and Père Joseph of the other book, for that matter. One does not ask—as one reads the harrowing narrative of Grandier's last days when the belated elevation of the priest's character is played off against the sadistic righteousness of his persecutors—whether it is Huxley the novelist or Huxley the essayist who is at work. His talents, however various and quite distinguishable they may appear in other work, achieve fusion or interplay as the shattered and repentant Urbain endures his last hours.[13] One has no great temptation to ask whether the writer is following or going beyond his documentation. Esthetically, at least, he has achieved the accents of truth.

One might say that Huxley's advantage in the two biographies is this: the inventor of the situations that challenge his skill is not himself but God or the vital force—or, as Huxley himself might say, the friction set up when primal unity falls into diversity. Hux-

ley's main task in these two books is not that of fabricating a
world; instead, his labor is the reconstitution of relationships as
they had once existed. The analysis of varieties of Christian religious experience puts into play erudition and cleverness that do
not (as elsewhere in Huxley) call attention to themselves. The
reader is likely to agree with Huxley that Grandier's tragedy *vis à
vis* that of the frantic nuns is a historical event rich in instruction
—provided—a very important proviso—he is convinced of the ap-
plicability of the insight which guides Huxley as he scans these
sections of human experience. This insight suggests that the tragedy of Grandier and the nuns stems from their failure to rise
above the false accounts of the religious life that they had accepted.

II Grey Eminence

The tragedy also appears in the earlier of the two biographies,
Grey Eminence, where it unfolds with a kind of quiet intensity.
Less sensational in its substance, the life of Père Joseph is still
quite interesting to one who has some degree of sympathy with
Huxley's conviction that the ultimate disaster of all men lies in
their failure to exploit what they are. Père Joseph, as is revealed
during Huxley's unrelenting pursuit of the mysterious and enig-
matic Capuchin, was not just another cleric who, like Grandier,
was indifferent to the high ranges of experience that Christian
mysticism offered. Grandier's choice of power and lechery was
made by a man who had never given a second thought to interior
prayer and to other techniques for purifying the spirit. Père Joseph, in contrast, was a man who knew full well what paths led to
mystical experience and sainthood.

Moreover, he was a man who aspired to follow these paths. Yet
he was—and here is the quieter but just as intense tragedy of
Grey Eminence—able to convince himself that political intrigue
on behalf of France was not a path opposed to the one which
Father Benet of Canfield and others had revealed to his mind in
his youth.[14] A career full of double-dealing, of actions that delayed by many years the conclusion of the bloody Thirty Years'
War, was not at odds with the service of God and an approach to
a full union with God. Or so Père Joseph persuaded himself. But
pursuits like Père Joseph's are—readers of Huxley are already
aware—full of danger. As Huxley points out in *Ends and Means*[15]

and elsewhere, the habit of compromise and connivance with evil may dull other faculties.

From Père Joseph's obtuseness at a crucial point comes his failure. As traced out in *Grey Eminence,* the failure is tangled with the many "necessary" comings and goings of Richelieu's "left hand" in a troubled Europe; the very arrival of the "grey eminence" could arouse fear. Père Joseph's travels, which reached from Paris to Ratisbon, Madrid, and Rome, finally produced a man who was as much a monster to himself as he was to those who feared him. He was a monster to others because of the moral evil—lies, the use of force, an indifference to suffering—to which he contributed. He was doubtless a monster to himself because he—unlike Grandier and most thoughtless workers of evil—knew rather clearly what he had turned away from: the practice of the presence of God.

One says advisedly: "he knew rather clearly." For Huxley contends that the particular mystical disciplines of prayer and meditation that Père Joseph had access to were flawed disciplines— flawed in such ways that, even if followed conscientiously, they would not allow a person to enjoy the full benefits of the "perennial philosophy." They were marred, as already noted, by the inferior instruction and guidance which he had from his early master, and by the pattern his mature life took—by the conviction that he could serve both God and Cardinal Richelieu. The "grey eminence" thought that he could "annihilate" the activities he undertook on behalf of Richelieu and France and preserve untarnished the relation to deity to which he aspired: "Given over to unannihilable activities, he came to be possessed, in spite of his daily practice of mental prayer, by a sense of bitterness and frustration. Visions, it is true, and prophetic revelations were still vouchsafed to him; but the unitive life of his early manhood was at an end; he had the dreadful certainty that God had moved away from him." [16]

Père Joseph was cut off from the "philosophy" that opens the way to a union with deity that is the same everywhere, whatever the differences among the religious structures where it takes place. Most mysticisms speak of the "emptying out" of the personality and of the culturally conditioned knowledge of the seeker, of the dark night he must journey through if he is to cancel all traces of himself, all traces of his individual awareness and passionate will.

Père Joseph's misfortune was to be uncritically immersed in the world which that savior and many other teachers wished to transform.

Such were the fatal errors of Père Joseph. It is useful, for a general understanding of Huxley's position, to underline the defects of a specifically *Christian* mysticism; for its errors define, in a negative way, the positive vision of what human powers can accomplish: the gospel—not new but just forgotten and overlooked in the twentieth century—which awaits the attention of each thoughtful man. For those who are not thoughtful, who will not listen, Huxley has no hope and, often, little sympathy. Christian mysticism had come to a focus on a deity who was an individual or had once been—an individual limited by a special history and a special time to one set of events. Branches of Christian mysticism —the mysticism, for example, expressed in the medieval treatise, *Cloud of Unknowing*—had expressed wiser insights. There is in all men a divine element of which they are unaware "because all their attention is fixed on the objects of craving and aversion. But, if they choose to 'die to self,' they can become aware of the divine element within them and, in it, experience God. For those who so desire and are prepared to fulfill the necessary conditions, the transcendent can in some way become immanent within the spark, at the apex of the higher will." [17] No counsel is given here that the human soul need, in its pilgrimage, linger at the foot of a particular cross in Palestine. Instead, the soul must court apprehensions of deity that are not visualized in images or expressed in words. Imageless, wordless illumination was mysticism pure and simple; away from it would drop such an adjective as "Christian."

Thus, the fatal error of Père Joseph's directors had been to inculcate in his mind the expectation that there was a unique way that mystics who happened to live in a *Christian* world had to follow. Instead, all human beings, simply because they were indeed human or "amphibious," had warrant to commence an ascent of a spiritual Mt. Carmel—a mountain open to all men, in the same way and without qualification. In meditating on the tragic destiny of Christ, a Christian could make a useful start, just as a Buddhist might in esteeming the heroic renunciation of the Buddha when he left the forest and returned to suffering mankind. But it was when a Christian persisted in his esteem for Jesus and regarded the figure of Christ as the terminus of the mystical journey that the Christian would find himself following a path that turned upon itself and indeed never went beyond a deadening concern with a particular human personality. Concern with personality—even though it might be that of a redeemer—could only, in Shelley's phrase, "stain the white radiance of eternity." If a seeker worked in the limiting way familiar to Père Joseph, he would never win a view of the indescribable light where the spirit of man is united with the unity of which man is an apparently diverse part.

Père Joseph never learned the real meaning of Jesus' utterance: "My Father is greater than I." [18] For Père Joseph, Jesus was a continuing model. Devoted to this model, Père Joseph never learned that there was a source of being and inspiration that was unstained by the marks of human personality—a source better than a god who became man, better even than a god who was a father to all mankind, for that god was concerned with the infinite value not only of the localized personality of his son, but also of the localized personalities and special histories of each created being who was only human. Gods who were saviors and gods who were fathers were but modes of apprehending deity and could serve as early milestones on the mystic's way. They were milestones that existed to be passed by and quite forgotten as one journeyed toward a deity to whom it would be an impiety to attribute human personality or, even, fatherly concern. The goal of the successful mystic was union with the superb indifference and the superb undiscussibility of a divine principle. Having reached the goal, the successful mystic could look back with sorrowing condescension at a mystic manqué like Père Joseph and at the order of Calvarian nuns which he founded to pray eternally at the foot of a cross. One could only smile sadly at the "grey eminence" and his nuns, wrestling with their all too human impressions as they kept their eyes resolutely fixed on the pierced hands and feet of a suffering god.

III *Estimates*

In conclusion, one can say of *Grey Eminence* and *The Devils of Loudun* that they are works in which Huxley chanced upon tasks that brought his wide-ranging concerns into a steady focus that allows one to see a relation among attitudes that elsewhere in Huxley's work are not clearly connected with each other. Elsewhere, the popularization of knowledge, satire, moralism—the drive to be an enlightener of man and more than just a novelist or an essayist—point beyond themselves and what they actually achieve. In *Grey Eminence* and *The Devils of Loudun* one sees what they point to.

In other works Huxley is often too much involved in "politics" as was Père Joseph. By "politics," of course, is meant more than the usual sense of the word; it includes the distractions of ambition and "image" that a novelist must be concerned with. But for once, in the two biographies, Huxley moves singularly free of the cleverness, facetiousness, and misplaced erudition that are the signs of his particular immersion in imperfect existence.

In the remaining work of Huxley there is much to admire. There is much more that is typical, with the familiar blend of merit and defect. But in that work there is nothing which reaches the eloquence, sincerity, and justice of many passages that, in *Grey Eminence* and *The Devils of Loudun,* recreate destinies which, until Huxley touched them, were objects of only antiquarian interest.

CHAPTER 7

Island

IN his last novel, *Island* (1962), Huxley takes up a form that he
might have returned to again had he lived to a more advanced
age. But, because of the position in his body of work which *Island*
occupies, it can be regarded as a kind of last will and testament.
And, suitably, *Island* is a full presentation of the almost irreducible tensions present in man, the "amphibious animal." In *Island*
the demonstration of the possible successes open to the human
animal is executed in terms of fiction rather than by means of
biographical investigations or protracted essays. And it is work
that, as will soon be clear, is a curious mixture of the various narrative genres in which Huxley had previously worked.

This observation gains some support from a simple summary of
the plot of *Island*. Unlike the chain of events in *Time Must Have
a Stop*, the doings of Will Farnaby, the hero in *Island*, offer scant
deference to matters of firm dramatic contrast and plot development that, one might observe, Huxley can manage when he
judges he has to. Farnaby, a journalist and *agent provocateur*,
lives in a time contemporary with Huxley's actual writing of his
novel, as·do most of Huxley's heroes. Farnaby is represented as
being a veteran of World War II; but any reader will see that he
is really a contemporary of Anthony Beavis in *Eyeless in Gaza*
(1936), who was a product of Edwardian culture and its particular kinds of hypocrisy and bigotry. And Will Farnaby cannot be
anything else, for Huxley, as usual, seeks a center of awareness
that will have something like his own range of response. In truth,
Huxley could not invent a consciousness in any depth that did not
contain the equivalents of his own impatient recollections of a
time when to be young was not "very heaven" but a sheer hell
constituted by the sexual hypocrisy, provincial nationalism, and
other defects of one's elders.

Furthermore, Will Farnaby is fleeing from a damaging sexual

experience, as do heroes like Walter Bidlake of *Point Counter Point* and Anthony Beavis of *Eyeless in Gaza*. Farnaby is, in fact, torn by the memory of two women: his "good" and sexually unsatisfactory wife who, unnerved by his cavalier dismissal of her, drove to her death; and his bedworthy mistress, Babs, who provided Farnaby with subhuman sexual ecstasy in a room illuminated by the changing light from an outdoor electric sign. The chamber of delight was now a hot red and now a green that was so nacreous and ghastly that the intertwined bodies of the lovers looked like corpses. In the green light "for ten hideous seconds Babs' rosy alcove became a womb of mud and, on the bed, Babs herself was corpse-colored, a cadaver galvanized into posthumous epilepsy." [1] After such sorrowful pleasures, the hero of *Island* wishes to have a year or so in which to write "seriously"; he is an easy victim of the temptations offered by an English press-lord to go to an island in the Indian Ocean (Pala) to help negotiate an oil treaty. The difficulty is simple: Pala is known to be rich in oil deposits, and yet, incomprehensibly, its rulers refuse to open their land to capitalistic exploitation.

On his way to Pala, Farnaby visits a nearby island ruled by an insufferable "tinpot" Hitler named Colonel Dipa—a visit that allows Huxley to parade once more the dubious benefits of the authoritarian state, in which order is imposed on misery but does nothing to alleviate it. His visit concluded, Farnaby sails for Pala, only to be wrecked on the shores of the almost magical island and to awaken on its sands to the sounds of mynah-birds saying, "Attention! Attention!" (thus is announced one of the main themes of the novel: the necessity for a precise response to whatever life offers). Farnaby is soon made welcome by Pala's peaceful inhabitants, who do not suspect that their sudden guest is the harbinger of the destruction that will soon overtake them.

Such are the somewhat stirring events which launch the novel; it is immediately becalmed. Will undergoes a protracted convalescence from his sea experience. He talks with many of the inhabitants of the island, who informed him of its origin and its customs.[2] Along with Will, the reader learns that the pleasant state of things on Pala is owing to the improbable meeting that took place in the nineteenth century between a Buddhist raja and the commonsense Scottish doctor he imported. Out of this meeting of the pragmatically effective West and the already religiously en-

lightened East came the modern Pala: a country that remains
abreast of modern technology but does not allow it to generate
the goals of life. As one of Farnaby's instructors remarks, "Why
would anyone want to exchange something rich and good and
endlessly interesting for something bad and thin and boring? We
don't feel any need for your speedboats or your television, your
wars and physical nonsense from Rome and Moscow." [3]

The teacher then explains the Tantrik version of Buddhist insight that guides Pala: "If you're a Tantrik, you don't renounce
the world or deny its value; you don't try to escape into a Nirvana
apart from life, as the monks of the Southern School do. No, you
accept the world, and you make use of it; you make use of everything you do, of everything that happens to you, of all the things
you see and hear and taste and touch, as so many means to your
liberation from the prison of yourself." [4]

The Tantrik-inspired wisdom of the old Raja lives on as a
counter-ferment to the yeast of the Western technology that is
constantly a threat to balance of life in Pala. In this wisdom there
are overtones of ancient scriptures and, one must confess, of
Kahlil Gibran: "Nobody needs to go anywhere else. We are all, if
we only knew it, already there." "The beings who are merely good
are not Good Beings; they are just pillars of society." "But Good
Being is in the knowledge of who in fact one is in relation to all
experiences . . . This is the only genuine yoga, the only spiritual
exercise worth practicing." [5]

This timeless wisdom enables the inhabitants of the island to
scan each possible importation of Western expertise and to decide
whether it will facilitate the triumph of the timeless "clear light"
or dim it. Thus, contraceptives have been enthusiastically accepted since they remove the element of risk and fear that often
marks early sexual experience. "Debonair" is, therefore, the only
word to describe the attitude of Farnaby's young nurse toward
her own sexual experience. The guilt and all else that have
marked the crypto-Edwardian Farnaby's experience of sex are
simply non-existent on Pala. It is *maithuna,* the yoga of love:
"What we're born with, what we experience all through infancy
and childhood, is a sexuality that isn't concentrated on the geni-
tals; it's a sexuality diffused throughout the whole organism.
Maithuna is the organized attempt to regain that paradise." [6] So
explains Ranga, a young man, to a bewildered Farnaby, who can-

not put behind him the possessiveness of Western sexuality. Methods of modern education—versions of which interested Huxley as early as an essay in *Proper Studies*[7]—have been enthusiastically adapted to meet the needs of Pala; the hypnopaedia of *Brave New World* has a partial continuation in the methods of suggestion used, but more conscious efforts are made to intensify (rather than manipulate only) the human powers of receptivity which are announced in the cry of the mynah-bird ("Attention! Attention!").[8]

Generally, life on Pala is indeed planned, but the plan represents attempts to recognize both the limitations and the untapped possibilities in each human being. A young woman, Susila, explains that means of deliverance are the "natural" endowment of each person, not a gift of divine aid erratically doled out to some mortals and denied others.

The point . . . is to get people to understand that we're not *completely* at the mercy of our memory and our phantasies. If we're disturbed by what's going on inside our heads, we can do something about it. It's all a question of being shown what to do and then practicing—the way one learns to write or play the flute. . . . This technique won't lead you to the discovery of your Buddha Nature [the unity of each man with the universe in which he exists]: but it may help you to prepare for that discovery. . . .[9]

Farnaby's contacts with various persons take place as a transparent means of demonstrating some excellence inherent in the Pala "solutions." Farnaby's chief cicerone is Dr. McPhail, who faces the death of his wife with dignity and resignation. McPhail says to his dying wife: "Let go now, let go. Leave it here, your old worn-out body, and go on. Go on, my darling, go into the Light, into the peace, into the living peace of the Clear Light. . . ."[10] From McPhail Farnaby also learns how the need for "building in" an element of risk in the peaceful island life is met by a requirment: all young persons must undergo a *rite de passage* that is of immense value for them, a perilous mountain climb. It is "the first stage of their initiation out of childhood into adolescence. An ordeal that helps them to understand the world they'll have to live in, helps them to realize the omnipresence of death, the essential precariousness of all existence."[11] The initiation is crowned by moments of revelation, the *moksha*-experience, the sensation of complete liberation. A scientifically controlled administration of hallucinogenic drugs gives the young people ranges of vision and suprapersonal awareness that are always lurking at the mystical end of the human spectrum, "a succession of beatific glimpses, an hour or two, every now and then, of enlightening and liberating grace." [12]

To the amazement and delight of Farnaby, who of course has hideous recollections of an English childhood, the family itself has been made humanly useful instead of remaining anthropophagous. (The family was canceled in the anti-utopias, *Brave New World* and *Ape and Essence*.) In Pala, children are not utterly committed to their parents and have other "families" to which they can go when the temperaments of their biological parents become oppressive. [13] Thus, the tyranny and the resultant hatred that Farnaby remembers from Edwardian England cannot be generated in Pala. Another beneficent modification of the family structure appears in the technological import of artificial insemination; a woman who wishes to vary the genetic equipment of her offspring is free to do so. [14]

Clouds drift across this sunny, eventless landscape: the evil, or uninstructed, wills of three persons, whose machinations provide what plot the novel contains: the Rani of the island, her son the young raja, and the dictator of the nearby island. Visions of oil and foreign wealth variously stir these persons. Wealth means sheer power to the dictator who, on the last two pages of the novel, forcibly unites Pala with his realm. [15] More deviously, for the Rani wealth spells support for her movement, the Crusade of the Spirit—a satiric reflection, one must suppose, of Huxley's memories of the once-celebrated movement in the 1930's of Moral Rearmament, in which (according to some critics) lush country house life, moral seriousness, and nascent fascism were blended by a leader named Dr. Frank Buchman. The Rani's movement has, however, structurally embarrassing overtones because it contains echoes of a theosophy that is first cousin to Huxley's own "Clear Light." [16]

One wonders how, on the level of intellectual discrimination, "perennial" philosophic sense is to be confidently winnowed from theosophic nonsense. One concrete standard that seems important for Huxley, in his satiric mockery of Moral Rearmament, is the

Rani's conviction that the supernatural—*any* supernatural—must be hand-in-glove with the moral discriminations that strike *her* as right and just. One learns elsewhere in the novel that the true beyond, the veridical "Clear Light," is to be spoken of only incidentally in a vocabulary that uses terms like "right" and "wrong." "'Right" and "wrong" are but illusions created by the endless dance of the god Shiva, who dances a dance of "endless becoming and passing away."

Dr. McPhail thus dismisses the kind of hope that misleads the Rani: hope for eternally binding moral verities: "What we would really like is a God who never destroys what he has created. Or if there must be pain and death, let them be meted out by a God of righteousness, who will punish the wicked and reward the good with everlasting happiness. But in fact the good get hurt, the innocent suffer. Then let there be a God who sympathizes and brings comfort." [17] The moral verities and the gods who sanction them can be no more than concessions to delusive human hope; the knell of this hope is not rung by death—a widespread impression —but by the *moksha*-experience.

The third cloud on the Pala horizon is the Rani's son Murugan, a particularly unattractive type in Huxley's eyes. To this young man, the oil money does not represent growth in power or support for a self-righteous moral crusade; the young raja aspires to a limitless hedonism. The young man's hedonism is oriented by homosexual patterns, and one might remark that Huxley's disapproving stance toward this defect is, in post-Wolfenden Report days, rather old-fashioned.[18] It is clear that such sexuality is for Huxley in a different category from the delights that contraceptive devices make possible for the heterosexual young of Pala —is, indeed, more reprehensible even than the mixture of attraction and repugnance that marks the sexuality of Farnaby, who was unable to love his wife or to enjoy his mistress. Farnaby's charming Pala nurse, for one, attempted to initiate her young prince into the satisfying, guiltless delights of pre-marital heterosexuality—but to no avail.[19] The Rani, as stupid as her Edwardian counterparts in other Huxley novels, cried out in moralistic terror and removed her son to a European environment where he was in fact free to develop his deplorable tendency.

These are the elements of surface interest contained in *Island*. As a novel, it is a tract—and more so than any other fiction Huxley wrote. The denouement is huddled into a few concluding pages; and the development of Farnaby's insights is much less convincing than, for example, Anthony Beavis' movement toward pacifism in *Eyeless in Gaza*. One might justly observe that Will Farnaby's mind is a blank album into which are pasted the various "programs" of Pala. That Farnaby finally detached himself from the English presslord and shares disaster with his newfound friends is not very moving; the novelist is the person who has really made the choice.

Esthetic estimate of the novel cannot rise very high; *Island* is not so much a novel as a mixture of most of the genres in which Huxley worked. But one must recognize that *Island* is less a novel than a utopian vision which brings into focus all that Huxley, in his later years, came to desire for man. Furthermore, it is a utopia of hope and is antithetical to the disturbing images that fill the pages of *Brave New World* and *Ape and Essence*. In this respect, it is the crown of the various and sometimes conflicting aspirations which his earlier writing records. It points to whatever concluding estimate one makes of the significance of Huxley's expression of his era and of Huxley's power to speak interestingly to later times.

CHAPTER 8

Conclusion

MANY points in the work of a writer as prolific as Huxley can seem pivotal—can suddenly have the air of being the hinge upon which the whole body of work swings. The principle that leads to an inclusive estimate of Huxley's variety must inform all he has done and yet be no more notably realized in one place than another. What one must seek is a pose or a gesture that can be recognized wherever it occurs. Here, quite possibly, one may be able to detect an element of continuity in Huxley's restless movement from novel to essay, from essay to biography, from biography to tract, and back again.

Huxley's mature estimate of the meaning of human personality and his detection of its limitations draw together many items that, lacking this clue, dangle. This estimate—worked out systematically in *The Perennial Philosophy* and elsewhere but embodied less systematically in works of fiction and casual essays—may be expressed thus: man must somehow be saved or improved. But what ordinarily goes under the heading *man* is not, in its own right, very estimable.

The formula receives a clear explication, for example, in the analysis of the experience of Père Joseph du Tremblay in *Grey Eminence*, in which the mysticism of Richelieu's aide is identified as a failed mysticism, one that will neither save nor improve the human being who practices it. Père Joseph's mysticism came to a halt in the blind alley of devotion to the person of Christ and a strenuous participation in Christ's sufferings as an individual. It is beyond this point that authentic, saving mysticism goes; it achieves its proper goal when the person is finally merged with the non-personal ground of all being and surrenders his identity there. The ground of all being—the One, primal unity, or what you will—cannot be discriminated or talked about. To it cannot be attributed such qualities as personality, fatherhood, justice, or mercy. And there is nothing in man's ordinary experience that prepares him to recognize what happens to him when he finally overtakes basic unity or (just as lucidly) basic unity finally overtakes him. All man can fall back on, if he wishes to comment on the experience, is a catalogue of negations; these are somewhat opposed to the positive and definite assertions that one is likely to employ when speaking of Christ and his passion.

Such a view of man and his crowning capacity is Huxley's mature assessment. That the assessment is hard to defend and that it is an aberration toward views that liberal-minded men of sense cannot accept are judgments that many readers will pronounce, for they will deplore the disappearance (never complete, however) of the streams of Huxley's wit, irreverence, and erudition into arid desert wastes of eclectic religiosity.

To pass such a judgment is one's privilege. It is less one's privilege to deny one's attention to this intellectual position, this "pivot," as it informs Huxley's work. For it bears the weight of Huxley's various activities; it is the mechanism on which swings freely and confidently a very great proportion of what Huxley has done. Even the work of the 1920's, mocking and often nihilistic, can be seen as a preparatory clearing action that lends support to part of the formula offered above: man is not worth saving. Before Huxley's insights matured, before his eclectic salvaging of essential truths found expression, Huxley could only express a profound nausea for man.

The nausea commences with man's basic processes of excretion; it moves on to the mechanics of copulation. Love, in the Huxley of the 1920's, is usually outright animality that overtakes persons who embrace, against their wills if they are superior, or in accordance with root-and-branch bestiality if they are more ordinary. Love—and all else that goes under the heading of "animality"— does not, in the early novels or in the essays, enhance human intelligence, and sensitivity; it is a negation of much that enlightened estimate calls "good" in mankind. To such seizure, art, poetry, music, and the other works of the intellect offer no real correction; they are merely palliatives that temporarily distract man from his brutish condition. For the less mature Huxley, man was—as American slang would put it—"no damn good."

It would be to psychologize in a way both disrespectful and impertinent to ask why the early Huxley came to these conclusions. (As was noted in the first chapter of this study, there is a contrast between Huxley as his close friends recalled him and Huxley as readers must know him; it is writer Huxley that is spoken of here.) Certainly, it would be only ingenious and untrue to seize upon a fact like Huxley's defective vision and to interpret the writer's disgust for man as a transcription of private envy and distaste. It is sufficient to note that the early satire of dismissal directed against man is not abandoned in later works; it remains as a stimulus to passages in which man is offered a transformation that he does not really deserve.

One might ask, holding in mind the richly embodied spectacle of human worthlessness in the novels and elsewhere, how indeed one can move to a concern *for* man in the face of the bleak evidence of his lack of worth. It is quite clear that Huxley's concern does not gather strength from his knowledge of the conventionally good; the "goodness" of some of the parents in *Point Counter Point* and in *Eyeless in Gaza* and of other secondary characters is freely acknowledged by the novelist—and dismissed as beside the main point. These persons have, it is true, escaped the worst follies; but their religious and moral simplicity are just their good fortune. How they have arrived at their basically naïve balances is empty of instruction for Huxley and for the readers he wishes to enlighten. The bulk of mankind—and this includes the "good"—are fools, actually or potentially.

From such sweeping derogation, how does Huxley move to the just as sweeping concern that leads him to investigate various possible avenues of salvation in the 1930's and later? Is the solipsistic consciousness that Huxley seems to share with many of his heroes broken in upon by the spectacle of sheer human misery, so that it is no longer laughable but rather a condition that must be altered? Or does the concern, as it takes shape, represent an emerging conviction that, as the ancient Gnostics would express it, there is in each man, however contemptible, a spark of divinity, a portion of the pure unity hideously mixed with inferior clay? If so, the divine spark must be freed. And superior persons must work in any way they can to advance this emancipation. This concern gives to the diversity of Huxley's work what unity it has.

I *The Huxleyan Balance*

Every man—some psychological determinists have suggested—wins the explicit set of ideas that his own nature destines him to accept. If some truth lies in this statement, one has the slight comfort of saying that Huxley's mature attitudes unite a contempt for mankind with an ardent desire to be of service to it. This statement at least underlines the limitations that many readers feel when they look in the mirror that Huxley holds up to life. A limner of man who has the impression, early and late, that man is not essentially interesting in his own right is likely to produce works with some of the shortcomings one can note in Huxley. What separates one man from another—his individual and often unique awareness—is less a precious mark to be industriously copied by the writer than a foolish tendency that must be exaggerated, so that every modicum of the folly inherent in cherishing one's individuality may be clearly perceived.

For the Huxley of *After Many a Summer Dies the Swan* and *Time Must Have a Stop*, the persons who achieve superior existence are those who have gone beyond the trammels of personality, the fear of death, and the constriction of being this man or that man at a particular time and place. All who plunge into the great sea of being, who merge with primal unity, have only one way to swim. Furthermore, in contrast with the graceful and easy motion that this sea makes possible, the ordinary movements of man must seem a floundering. And the depiction of such floundering—in novels and in essays that make an analysis of human behavior—is marked, in Huxley, by a kind of impatient reportage, lively when the sheer grotesqueness of human folly amuses the writer and dull when the writer is oppressed by the basic tediousness of human behavior.

It may be added that Huxley's insight into man—that he is the creature who must supplement or fulfill his animal and rational natures by some sort of vision that is the same for all who enjoy it—is peculiarly limiting to a novelist. With a truly Gnostic or Buddhist accent, Huxley can speak of the elements that go to make up an individual as signs of the "fall" of unity into diversity and the subsequent "fall" of man from instinctual nescience into rational discriminations. Disconcertingly, one realizes that it is on these two levels—that of instinct and that of rational discrimination—that human character moves. On these levels most novelists find their subjects and consider it worth their while to note the particular interplay between the animal and the rational that is offered by a chosen personage.

Concerning the crown of existence—beatific vision, the sense of the "Clear Light"—the novelist can say very little; he works with words; and words are the creation of the second level of existence, the rational or the specifically human. Most novelists—one may say a little cynically—have had the good fortune not to have been struck by the beatific vision and are not deeply curious about it. Thus limited in their interests, most novelists can give a careful attention to life that comprises the animal and rational (or somewhat rational) levels. The novelists can, thanks to a limitation of awareness that they are unconscious of, deal with the existences of other men with a deep curiosity and even compassion since those existences are identical with the existence of the writer who notes them down. This novelistic compassion is quite unlike the compassion of the Buddha, who has seen beyond human good and evil, beyond desire and its evil results. This latter compassion, noble as it may be, cancels the worth, the intrinsic interest and value of the human object. And this compassion was deeply attractive to Huxley; it is the explanation if not the model of Huxley's own attitude toward the characters he drew.

The presence of this sort of compassion may be one of the reasons why most of Huxley's novels do not move forward and express the impetus of a given situation and the interplay of the different persons involved in the situation. Huxley's novels usually move forward thanks to the appearance of new and often outré events and the arbitrary appearance of new and odd persons. The characters in his novels are members of an amusing and sometimes instructive but seldom touching parade.

One may make an estimate of Huxley's skill as an essayist without quite such a curious attention to the link between his developed convictions and his execution of them. In his essays, Huxley recorded a general twentieth-century need not to cancel the past but to make an inspection of it that would render it available for modern needs. Like T. S. Eliot, Huxley sought a "usable past." Like André Malraux in his role of art historian, Huxley regarded the past as a great museum in which modern man is obligated to wander for edification. With wide-ranging curiosity, Huxley went back and forth over the arts, literature, and records of history, always in search of some chance clue that would illuminate the present, always hopeful of turning up a past gesture that might be useful for imitation or, by its very strangeness, offer defining contrast.

But Huxley was not a detached culture historian for whom the chief duty is that of describing accurately some ancient complex of buildings or a battered mosaic. Explicit or implicit in Huxley's discussions of Renaissance palaces or Indian and Mexican temples was always this question: what do these ancient forms tell modern man about *his* forms? Various as Huxley's interests were, it is significant that—with the crucial exception of his attention to the very long history of mysticism—he found Renaissance and post-Renaissance times the most suggestive; they were the true matrices of modern man. The magnificence of Renaissance courts and their humanism, intellectually daring and morally reckless; the pretensions and the hopes of seventeenth-century religion (particularly in France); the cold light of the eighteenth-century day (quite different from the "Clear Light" of mystical insight, Huxley finally says); the imbalance and diabolist extremes of the nineteenth century—all these past experiences offered Huxley chances to comprehend the nearby and the more distant forces that had gone into the making of twentieth-century man.

This desire to win instruction is a strength in Huxley; but it leads, as in some of his remarks on the art of painting, to overhasty reductions of the work of art to what the work of art says—says about its own time, says to modern man. In an era when the temptation is to create difficult gulfs between questions of form and questions of meaning, one can find Huxley's bland indifference to this division somewhat endearing. For art, music, and architecture—as well as literature—speak to Huxley not of themselves but of man. They speak directly of the persons who created the palaces, the paintings, or the motets that win his attention; they speak of the periods that found partial expression in the fugues of Bach or the fantasies of Goya; they speak, finally and most insistently, of Huxley's own era. (It would be beside Huxley's point to observe that this last intention was certainly not in the mind of Bach, Goya, or any other past artist.)

The early and late essays, specifically observed, would, if traced out, indicate the variation that has been traced in the fiction.

What Huxley specifically makes of an Indian temple in the early *Jesting Pilate*[1] is quite different from his prolonged meditation on an imprudent French priest in *The Devils of Loudun*[2] or on the relation between an Asia Minor deity and the alphabet;[3] and that difference is to be explained by reference to the intellectual development already traced in Chapter Two. It is enough to remark here that Huxley's curiosities were the opposite of encyclopedic; from his studies and from those of others—particularly from those of modern sociologists, psychologists, and physiologists—Huxley garnered curious circumstance not for its own sake but for the well-being of those who read. With a slight alteration of phrase, the last sentence is an adequate description of his fiction also.

Much modern taste—a little inconsistently, perhaps—accepts a desire to be useful as a proper one in a man's performance of the role of social philosopher (a part Huxley often played) and reprobates such a desire when it is part of the fabric of a novel. Future times may be less queasy than this era about didactic elements in imaginative works. If, however, this uneasiness about direct exhortation in such works is inherited by later generations, Huxley's novels (and those of his imaginative works classified as essays) may be eclipsed. Both novel and essay, as Huxley elaborates these forms, are inescapably didactic, as are the two biographies in which the history of the past is set to work milling the grain of the present and the near future.

II *Conclusion*

To the assessment just completed, one might add that Huxley's chance to survive in the general libraries that future Anglo-Saxon readers will draw on is open to question. But Huxley must always be regarded as a useful transcriber and interpreter of the uncertainties of the first half of the twentieth century: Where lies human guidance? In whose hands? In the hands of the men who work in the exact and inexact sciences? Or should one turn to other men, whose labor preserves and interprets the fragments of a very ancient wisdom? To none of these questions does Huxley, interestingly enough, give flat answers. There are times when Huxley falls in with the majority opinion of his time and seems to give the nod to scientific endeavor; *here* lies guidance. Yet there are other instances when Huxley offers a resounding denial to science or, better, scientific omnicompetence.

Another question repeatedly asked in this century concerns the connection between the intellectually gifted person and the society in which he lives. If he stands apart, is he not guilty of the "treason of the clerks"? Yet if he does not, what dangers he runs into! Again, as with the other issue, Huxley sometimes washes his hands of current and burning questions and retires to studies that are at a distance from lacerating battles. But at other moments, Huxley speaks as a committed man—as committed, that is, as a person of his gifts and insights can be.

In his considerable range of answers, Huxley is revealing of the ebb and flow of hope in his times. He was—with an effect of illumination that was strong for some of his contemporaries and that, one may imagine, will be doubly strong for later students of his time—a warrior in many of its characteristic battles. He never won, and he was never defeated; and here he shared the lot of many of his peers. And Huxley returned to inconclusive contests without asking on what terms he had fought in a previous skirmish and earned success and defeat.

If one narrows the light to focus on Huxley, it can be made out that Huxley was, unlike persons who are more aware of the supposed demands of consistency, less careful of preserving himself and his integrity, artistic and intellectual, than eager to win a particular phase of the battles of the twentieth century as he understood them. His way of conducting the necessary warfare was not, it is obvious, the only way or even the best way. But he did what was possible for him. His acid sincerity and his strategies that sometimes discredited previous positions of his own indicate a nerve and a persistence not often found in a man whose basic literary stance kept him at some distance from the mass of men.

Notes and References

Unless otherwise noted, the references to Huxley's works apply to the uniform edition published by Chatto and Windus, London.

Chapter One

1. *Aldous Huxley, 1894–1963, A Memorial Volume,* ed. Julian Huxley (London, 1965). This book will hereafter be referred to as *A.H.*
2. Cf. Stephen Spender's remarks in *A.H.,* p. 19.
3. *Point Counter Point,* p. 107.
4. *A.H.* (Gervas Huxley), p. 58.
5. *Ibid.* (Juliette Huxley), p. 42.
6. See Cyril Bibby, *T. H. Huxley, Scientist, Humanist and Educator* (London, 1959), pp. 67–88.
7. T. H. Huxley, *Critiques and Addresses* (London, 1873), p. 51.
8. *A.H.* (Leonard Woolf), p. 35.
9. *Ibid.* (Gervas Huxley), p. 57.
10. *Eyeless in Gaza,* pp. 73–77.
11. *A.H.* (Juliette Huxley), p. 42; (Gervas Huxley), p. 58.
12. *Ibid.* (Gervas Huxley), p. 59. *The Art of Seeing* (New York, 1952) contains Huxley's account of his later efforts to deal with his problem.
13. *A.H.* (Kenneth Clark), p. 15.
14. *Ibid.* (Naomi Mitchison), pp. 51ff.; (Raymond Mortimer) pp. 135ff.
15. John Atkins, *Aldous Huxley* (London, 1956), p. 25.
16. *A.H.* (Sybille Bedford), p. 140.
17. *Ibid.* (Gervas Huxley), p. 56.
18. *Ibid.* (Raymond Mortimer), p. 135.
19. *Ibid.* (T. S. Eliot), p. 30. Huxley's volumes of poetry are as follows: *The Burning Wheel* (1916); *The Defeat of Youth* (1918); *Leda* (1920); *Selected Poems* (1925); *Arabia Infelix* (1929); *The Cicadas* (1931).
20. See the comments in *A.H.,* pp. 36, 39, 52, 75, 115.
21. *Ibid.* (Juliette Huxley), p. 40.
22. *Ibid.* (Naomi Mitchison), p. 53.

23. For an account of Garsington, the probable model, see Lady Ottoline Morrell, *Ottoline,* ed. Robert Gathorne-Hardy (London, 1963), pp. 20–36.

24. Osbert Sitwell, *Laughter in the Next Room* (Boston, 1948), p. 25.

25. *A.H.* (Stephen Runciman), pp. 27–29.

26. Robert H. Ross, *The Georgian Revolt: 1910–1922* (Carbondale, Ill., 1965), pp. 167, 169, 170, 171, 178, 181. For Huxley's own account of his apprenticeship years, see "The Art of Fiction, XXIV, Aldous Huxley," *Paris Review,* No. 23 (1960), p. 63.

27. *A.H.* (Juliette Huxley), p. 39; (Humphry Osmond), p. 115; (Sybille Bedford), pp. 138–43.

28. *A.H.* (Sybille Bedford), p. 142.

29. Atkins, *op. cit.,* p. 25.

30. Harry T. Moore, *The Intelligent Heart: the Life of D. H. Lawrence* (rev. ed., New York, 1962), p. 263.

31. Edward Nehls, *D. H. Lawrence: a Composite Biography* (Madison, Wis., 1959), III, 116.

32. Moore, *op. cit.,* p. 512. Huxley had experience of censorship difficulties himself. His collection of stories, *Brief Candles* (1930), as well as *Point Counter Point* (1928), was banned in Ireland (*New York Times,* July 12, 1930). Later, *Eyeless in Gaza* (1936) was impounded by the Censorship Board of Australia (*New York Times,* October 1, 1936).

33. Nehls, *op. cit.,* III, 436, 442.

34. *The Letters of D. H. Lawrence,* ed. and with an introduction by Aldous Huxley (New York, 1932).

35. Aldous Huxley, *Beyond the Mexique Bay,* p. 311–14.

36. *A.H.* (Christopher Isherwood), p. 156.

37. Aldous Huxley, *The Art of Seeing* (New York, 1942). Dr. Bates's own theories are summarized in chap. ii, pp. 24–40.

38. For an account of the Huxley-Heard relationship, see William York Tindall, "The Trouble with Aldous Huxley," *American Scholar,* XI (Autumn, 1942), 452–64. For Heard's own account, see Gerald Heard, "The Poignant Prophet," *Kenyon Review,* XXVII (Winter, 1965), 49–70.

39. *A.H.* (Leonard Woolf), p. 35.

40. *Ibid.* (Christopher Isherwood), p. 154.

41. *Ibid.* (Anita Loos), p. 95.

42. Huxley wrote or collaborated on scenarios for *Pride and Prejudice, Jane Eyre, Madame Curie,* and *A Woman's Vengeance,* the last based on *The Gioconda Smile.*

43. *Jesting Pilate,* pp. 261–70.

44. *A.H.* (Sybille Bedford), p. 139.

45. *Ibid.* (Julian Huxley), p. 24. Cf. the remarks quoted in the *New York Times,* May 21, 1959.

46. *Ibid.* (Anita Loos), pp. 91–93.

47. *Ibid.* (Anita Loos), p. 94.

48. *Ibid.* (Humphry Osmond), p. 118. Cf. Huxley's own account in *The Door of Perception* (New York, 1954), pp. 16ff. For Huxley's own comment at a later date on the benefits and limitations of the experience, see "The Art of Fiction, XXIV, Aldous Huxley," *Paris Review,* No. 23 (1960), 66–69.

49. *A.H.* (Gerald Heard), p. 104.

50. *Ibid.* (Julian Huxley), p. 25; (Harrison Brown), p. 107; (Humphry Osmond), p. 121.

51. In 1959 Huxley received an award from the American Academy of Letters (*New York Times,* April 1, 1959). In 1962 he was elected a Companion of Literature of the British Royal Society of Literature (*New York Times,* June 8, 1962).

52. Huxley wrote an introduction to a book written by his second wife, Laura Archera Huxley: *You Are Not the Target* (1963). The book treats matters closely related to Huxley's own interests.

53. E.g., the treatment of Maine de Biran in "Variations on a Philosopher" in *Themes and Variations* (1950), where topics already explored in *The Perennial Philosophy* (1945) are taken up again.

Chapter Two

1. For samples of such criticism, see the following: Edwin B. Burgum, "Aldous Huxley and His Dying Swan," in his *The Novel and The World's Dilemma* (New York, 1947), pp. 140–56; and William Y. Tindall, "The Trouble with Aldous Huxley;" *American Scholar,* XI (Autumn, 1942), 452–64.

2. Cf. the conclusion to "Pascal" in *Do What You Will* (1929), p. 309.

3. *Point Counter Point,* p. 601.

4. For an account of these difficulties, see Kenneth Scott Latourette, *Christianity in a Revolutionary Age: The Nineteenth Century in Europe: the Protestant and Eastern Churches* (New York, 1959), II, 295–310.

5. Bishop R. H. Codrington, *The Melanesians* (New Haven, 1957).

6. *Do What You Will,* pp. 119f.

7. *Ibid.,* pp. 211f.

8. "Variations on a Baroque Tomb" in *Themes and Variations,* p. 170.

9. "The Education of an Amphibian" in *Tomorrow and Tomorrow and Tomorrow* (New York, 1956), pp. 1ff. The quotations elsewhere in this chapter are from this edition.

10. *Island* (New York, 1962), p. 108. The quotations elsewhere in this chapter are from this edition.

11. *The Perennial Philosophy* (New York, 1945), pp. 188f. The quotations elsewhere in this chapter are from this edition.

12. *Ibid.*, p. 23.

13. *Island*, p. 196.

14. *The Perennial Philosophy*, pp. 172, 182.

15. *Ibid.*, pp. 141, 168.

16. *Tomorrow and Tomorrow and Tomorrow*, pp. 193ff.

17. E.g., *The Doors of Perception* (New York, 1963), p. 34.

18. *The Perennial Philosophy*, pp. 182, 228.

19. *Ibid.*, p. 194. Cf. *Tomorrow and Tomorrow and Tomorrow*, pp. 193, 200.

20. *The Perennial Philosophy*, pp. 228ff.

21. These may be listed here: *Ends and Means* (1937), *The Art of Seeing* (1943), *The Perennial Philosophy* (1946), *Science, Liberty, and Peace* (1947), *The Doors of Perception* (1954), *Heaven and Hell* (1956), *Brave New World Revisited* (1959), and *Literature and Science* (1963). Those which take up themes treated in connection with discussion of other works may be briefly characterized here. *The Art of Seeing* and *The Doors of Perception* consider the precise aid that certain scientific discoveries offer man: *The Art of Seeing* is concerned with the sharpening of physical vision, and *The Doors of Perception* treats mescalin and its power to sharpen both physical and mental perceptions. Three books—*Ends and Means, Science, Liberty and Peace,* and *Brave New World Revisited*—treat various aspects of the modern world, usually with repetitive consistency. *Heaven and Hell* takes up the clues that art and literature offer to the states of being that the conventional words in the title refer to. *Literature and Science* expresses Huxley's habitual view that the tensions between what C. P. Snow called "the two cultures" can be resolved only by a perception of their mutual dependency.

Chapter Three

1. Huxley's stories, all written in the first decade and a half of his writing career, were collected under the following titles: *Limbo* (1920); *Mortal Coils* (1922); *Little Mexican* (1924); *Two or Three Graces* (1926); and *Brief Candles* (1930.)

2. The essays of this period are collected under the following titles: *On the Margin* (1923); *Along the Road* (1925); *Proper Studies* (1927); *Do What You Will* (1928); *Vulgarity in Literature* (1930); and *Music at Night* (1931).

3. The titles of the volumes of poems are as follows: *The Burning*

Wheel (1916); *The Defeat of Youth* (1918); *Leda* (1920); *Arabia Infelix* (1929); and *The Cicadas* (1931).

4. E.g., the poems of Francis Chelifer in *Those Barren Leaves,* pp. 120, 123, 125, and 145; and the poems of Sebastian Barnack, pp. 3, 30, 51, 180, and 241 in *After Many a Summer Dies the Swan.*

5. Examples of Huxley's persistent attacks on respectable and conventional assumptions abound in the short stories. The unremitting venom of Huxley's hostility may be sampled in two stories, "Chawdron" and "The Claxtons" (*Brief Candles,* 1930), in which pretensions to spirituality are shown up for what they are: masks for carnality or oblique expressions of constipation.

6. For a cavalier dismissal of Bennett's importance as a model, see "Chawdron" in *Brief Candles,* p. 7.

7. *Those Barren Leaves,* p. 53. "Nuns at Luncheon" (*Mortal Coils*) reproduces the conversation of two literary persons who contemplate making a story of a tragic incident. The basic casualness and the unconcern of the two persons towards their arts cast light on the variations in tone in Huxley's own early novels.

8. An attempt is made in *Antic Hay* to present the troubles the poor encounter in pursuit of a livelihood (pp. 64–69), but the sufferings of the poor are quickly caught up in the self-conscious mockery of the educated. "Fairy Godmother," in *Two or Three Graces* (1926), is also representative of Huxley's treatment of the financially deprived; benevolence toward the needy is shown to be a kind of vanity since the poor in the story exist as occasions for the display of this vanity and not as objects of interest in their own right.

9. This can be sampled in the treatment of the parents of the remarkable child in "Young Archimedes" (*Little Mexican*) and of the servants in the later novel, *Time Must Have a Stop.* One cannot fail to be struck, furthermore, by the casual dismissal given Negroes and Jews in Huxley's fiction. This may be sampled in *Antic Hay,* p. 294; *Those Barren Leaves,* pp. 107, 133; *Brave New World,* p. 99; *Time Must Have a Stop,* p. 51. See also the reference to Africans in "Leda," *Verses and a Comedy,* p. 36.

10. Rebecca West, *The Strange Necessity* (Garden City, 1928), pp. 215ff.

11. See *Joyce the Artificer: Two Studies of Joyce's Method* by Aldous Huxley and Stuart Gilbert (London, 1952).

12. *Antic Hay,* pp. 56ff.

13. E.g., Miss Thriplow's recollection of a dead cousin is suggested to her by the odor of a crushed bayleaf in *Those Barren Leaves,* pp. 48–50.

14. One of the most striking examples appears at the musical soiree of Lady Edward Tantamount in *Point Counter Point,* chaps. iii to v,

where each conversation is ironically at odds with other interchanges that take place.

15. The presentation of Miss Thriplow's devious character in *Those Barren Leaves* demonstrates the value of this kind of counterpoint. Her assumption of various roles has the accompaniment of her mental comment on the charades she plays (e.g., *Those Barren Leaves*, pp. 5–12, 57f.). A more serious example of the same effect appears in chap. i of *Point Counter Point*, where Walter Bidlake makes mental comment on the shoddy sentences he utters to his mistress.

16. An irreducible texture of cross-purpose appears in the chatter of Lucy Tantamount, the artist John Bidlake, and his former mistress, Mrs. Betterton, in *Point Counter Point*, pp. 62–68. They appear to be talking to each other, but they are actually talking to themselves.

17. In chaps. viii and x of *Point Counter Point* the conversation around the table at Sbisa's restaurant is a telling display of clever people unable to profit from each other's presence—a recurrent theme in Huxley's fiction.

18. Huxley's tendency to wreathe a simple action with an abundance of impressive but eventually irrelevant information about art, cultural contrasts, and chance observations on human behavior can be sampled in "Little Mexican" and "Young Archimedes" (*Little Mexican*), where ironic chains of event are almost lost in an undergrowth of comment which the knowing author cannot suppress. It is just to observe that there are other stories in which Huxley drives with praiseworthy economy toward his narrative point. Such success can be sampled in "The Tillotson Banquet" (*Cornhill Magazine*, n.s. M.S.L. [January, 1921], 90–109) and "Fairy Godmother" in *Two or Three Graces* (1926).

19. *Crome Yellow*, pp. 83–98.

20. The work of Gombauld and all the other artists who crop up in Huxley's fiction is somehow beyond Cubism and Abstractionism and seems to aim at a fusion between form and statements about man. Gombauld in *Crome Yellow* (p. 75), Lypiatt in *Antic Hay* (pp. 74–80), and Rampion in *Point Counter Point* (pp. 286–91) all work in the same atelier. That Huxley is merely amused by Lypiatt and impressed by Rampion represents the early Huxley's usual ambivalent attitude toward human effort, which may be laughed at in one context and esteemed in another.

21. "Eupompus Gave Splendor to Art by Numbers" (*Limbo*).

22. *Crome Yellow*, p. 40.

23. *Ibid.*, pp. 54–58.

24. *Ibid.*, p. 45.

25. *Ibid.*, pp. 20f.

26. *Antic Hay*, pp. 225–48. The "hay" in the title is a reference to an old, jig-like dance.

27. "Hubert and Minnie" (*Little Mexican*) is a representative sample of Huxley's unfeeling depiction of human efforts to break out of the circle of social restrictions placed upon the expression of sexuality.

28. *Antic Hay*, pp. 26–30.

29. *Ibid.*, pp. 122f.

30. *Ibid.*, p. 166.

31. *Ibid.*, p. 226.

32. *Ibid.*, pp. 160f.

33. *Crome Yellow*, pp. 20, 178, 188.

34. *Antic Hay*, p. 81. The title of the German translation of *Those Barren Leaves* goes to the heart of the matter and is, quite simply, *Parallelen der Liebe* (Frankfurt, 1961).

35. *Point Counter Point*, pp. 228f., 601. For an actual parallel to this situation, see F. A. Lea, *John Middleton Murry* (London, 1959), p. 116.

36. *Those Barren Leaves*, p. 109; *Point Counter Point*, pp. 181f.

37. *Antic Hay*, pp. 18–30.

38. *Ibid.*, pp. 44–48.

39. *Point Counter Point*, p. 238.

40. *Eyeless in Gaza*, p. 104.

41. *Antic Hay*, pp. 218, 249.

42. Italian locations are often the subjects of the essays that Huxley was writing during this period. In *Along the Road* (1925) there are essays on a monastery named Montesenario and a model town, Sabbioneta. There are also accounts of the Palio at Siena and of Pietramala, a village in the Appenines.

43. *Those Barren Leaves*, p. 18.

44. *Ibid.*, pp. 44f.

45. *Ibid.*, pp. 83–174.

46. *Ibid.*, pp. 319–29.

47. *Ibid.*, pp. 167, 199.

48. *Ibid.*, p. 215.

49. Miss Thriplow's various meditations suggest that the art of writing fiction is the art of amusing and distracting readers rather than a careful revelation of what the author essentially is or hopes. These theories may be sampled in *Those Barren Leaves*, pp. 49, 53, 208f.

50. *Those Barren Leaves*, pp. 25f., 303f.

51. One must observe that the habits of composition outlined here are not altered in later work. In a much later work, *After Many a Summer Dies the Swan* (1939), the novel commences centered in the consciousness of a young Englishman named Jeremy Pordage. But after seven chapters, this young man's awareness is abandoned for persons whose minds are useful in later stages of the argument Huxley is unfolding.

52. "Happily Ever After" in *Limbo*.

53. "Fard" in *Little Mexican*.

54. The bulk of the narrative in *The Genius and the Goddess* (1955) is John Rivers' first-person account of a past love affair.

55. *Those Barren Leaves*, pp. 50, 80.

56. The protagonist of "Half-Holiday" (*Two or Three Graces*) has a speech defect. So has Brian Foxe in *Eyeless in Gaza*.

57. "Nuns at Luncheon" (*Mortal Coils*).

58. *Those Barren Leaves*, pp. 343ff.

59. *Ibid.*, pp. 343f.

60. *Ibid.*, pp. 362–80.

61. *Brave New World* (New York, 1958), p. vii.

62. See "The Substitutes for Religion" in *Proper Studies*, pp. 207–29.

63. *Proper Studies*, pp. 82–85.

64. *Point Counter Point*, pp. 44, 48.

65. See "Water Music" in *On the Margin*, p. 39; and "Music at Night" in *Music at Night*, p. 43.

66. See "Breughel" in *Along the Road*, p. 133; and "Meditation on El Greco" in *Music at Night*, p. 53.

67. There are, for example, calculated contrapuntal effects in "Nuns at Luncheon" in *Mortal Coils* (1922).

68. *Point Counter Point*, p. 92.

69. *Ibid.*, pp. 41ff.

70. *Ibid.*, pp. 1–22.

71. *Ibid.*, pp. 492f.

72. *Ibid.*, pp. 305f, 363f.

73. *Ibid.*, pp. 409f.

74. *Ibid.*, p. 107.

75. *Ibid.*, p. 238.

76. *Ibid.*, p. 584.

77. *Ibid.*, p. 578.

78. *Ibid.*, p. 157.

79. *Ibid.*, p. 270. For a similar vein of comment on the stupidity of Satanism, see the comments on Dostoyevsky's heroes—among them, Stavrogin of *The Possessed*—in *Do What You Will*, pp. 173f.

80. *Point Counter Point*, p. 290.

81. "Holy Face" and "Pascal" in *Do What You Will*.

82. *Point Counter Point*, pp. 246, 302.

83. *Ibid.*, p. 596.

84. *Ibid.*, p. 45.

85. *Proper Studies*, p. 9.

Chapter Four

1. E.g., see Arnold Toynbee's use of the novel in *A Study of History* (London, 1954), IX, 203, 612–14.
2. *Brave New World,* p. 45.
3. *Ibid.,* p. 53.
4. *Ibid.,* pp. 21ff.
5. *Ibid.,* p. 5.
6. *Ibid.,* p. 27.
7. *Ibid.,* p. 30.
8. *Ibid.,* p. 22.
9. *Ibid.,* p. 33 (Centrifugal Bumble Puppy), p. 51 (Obstacle Golf).
10. *Ibid.,* pp. 47f.
11. *Ibid.,* p. 103.
12. *Ibid.,* p. 193.
13. *Ibid.,* p. 100.
14. *Ibid.,* p. 43.
15. *Ibid.,* pp. 88.
16. *Ibid.,* pp. 259f.
17. *Ibid.,* p. 244.
18. See the foreword to *Brave New World,* written in 1946 (New York, 1958), p. viii.
19. *Ibid.*
20. *Ibid.,* p. vii. *Brave New World Revisited* (1958) is an extensive discussion of the implications of the novel, as understood from Huxley's later point of view.
21. *Beyond the Mexique Bay,* pp. 311–14.
22. E.g., chap. iii in *Brave New World* where the technique is pushed farther than it is in *Point Counter Point.*
23. "Swift" in *Do What You Will,* pp. 93–106.

Chapter Five

1. It is significant that Huxley no longer wrote short stories at this time. Full-scale demonstrations of convictions do not—in Huxley, at any rate—harmonize with the shorter narrative form.
2. *Eyeless in Gaza,* pp. 42ff.
3. *Ibid.,* pp. 590ff.
4. *Ibid.,* pp. 278f.
5. *Ibid.,* p. 8.
6. *Ibid.,* p. 12.
7. *Ibid.,* pp. 549–57.
8. *Ibid.,* p. 552.

9. *Ibid.*, p. 377.
10. *Ibid.*, pp. 616f.
11. *Ibid.*, pp. 169, 620.
12. *Ibid.*, pp. 583–89.
13. E.g., *ibid.*, pp. 84, 139, 171, 228.
14. *Ibid.*, p. 572.
15. *Ibid.*, p. 586.
16. *Ibid.*, pp. 289ff.
17. *Ibid.*, p. 604.
18. *Ibid.*, p. 522.
19. *Ibid.*, pp. 450, 477.
20. *Ibid.*, pp. 557ff.
21. *Point Counter Point*, p. 155.
22. *Eyeless in Gaza*, p. 327.
23. *Ibid.*, p. 330.
24. *Beyond the Mexique Bay*, p. 123.
25. *Eyeless in Gaza*, pp. 152ff.
26. W. B. Yeats, *Collected Poems* (New York, 1950), p. 255.
27. *Island*, p. 152.
28. "Swift" in *Do What You Will*, pp. 93ff.
29. *Eyeless in Gaza*, pp. 250, 463 (Brian); pp. 271, 308f. (Hugh).
30. *Point Counter Point*, pp. 238–44.
31. *Antic Hay*, pp. 142f.
32. *Eyeless in Gaza*, p. 82.
33. *Ibid.*, p. 290.
34. *Ibid.*, p. 278.
35. *Ibid.*, pp. 348, 483f.
36. *Antic Hay*, p. 156.
37. *Eyeless in Gaza*, pp. 481–85.
38. The relation of the young man Rivers to the "goddess" in *The Genius and the Goddess* (1955) is Huxley's attempt to trace a redemptive pattern in a sexual relationship.
39. *Ends and Means*, pp. 307ff. See also *Tomorrow and Tomorrow and Tomorrow* (New York, 1962), pp. 98f.
40. *After Many a Summer Dies the Swan*, p. 108. The title of the novel is drawn from the opening lines of Tennyson's "Tithonus," a poem which concerns a man who asks for eternal life and fails to ask for eternal youth also.

> The woods decay, the woods decay and fall,
> The vapors weep their burthen to the ground,
> Man comes and tills the field and lies beneath,
> And after many a summer dies the swan.

41. See, for example, chap. vii and viii in *Ends and Means*.
42. A useful and characteristic analysis of what "amphibious being"

comes to appears in the essay, "Adonis and the Alphabet," in *Tomorrow and Tomorrow and Tomorrow* (1956).

43. *The Perennial Philosophy* (New York, 1945), pp. 161–74.

44. *After Many a Summer Dies the Swan*, pp. 110f.

45. *Ibid.*, p. 120.

46. *Ibid.*, p. 100.

47. *Ibid.*, p. 144.

48. *Ibid.*, pp. 148–52.

49. *Ibid.*, pp. 162f.

50. Bruno Rontini in *Time Must Have a Stop* takes the same view of the sexual enslavement of Eustace Barnack.

51. *After Many a Summer Dies the Swan*, pp. 226f.

52. *Ibid.*, p. 157.

53. *Jesting Pilate*, pp. 261–70.

54. *After Many a Summer Dies the Swan*, p. 48. This insistence on Dr. Obispo's Levantine qualities leads one to remark that Huxley applies to "Levantines," Jews, and Negroes various stereotypes: acumen and libidinousness for the Jews and Levantines; uninhibited animal sexuality for the Negroes.

55. *Ibid.*, p. 141. Cf. *Point Counter Point*, pp. 159f.

56. *Ibid.*, pp. 236f.

57. *Ibid.*, pp. 198f, 205.

58. *Henry IV, Part One*, Act V, scene 4, line 82.

59. Cf. chap. ix, "War," in *Ends and Means*.

60. *Time Must Have a Stop*, p. 284.

61. *Ibid.*, pp. 270–305.

62. *Ibid.*, pp. 298f.

63. *Ibid.*, pp. 38–61.

64. *Ibid.*, p. 66.

65. *Ibid.*, p. 69.

66. *Ibid.*, p. 87.

67. *Ibid.*, p. 36.

68. *Ibid.*, p. 292.

69. *Ibid.*, p. 176.

70. *Ibid.*, p. 171.

71. *Ibid.*, p. 266.

72. *Ibid.*, p. 176.

73. *Ibid.*, pp. 96f.

74. *After Many a Summer Dies the Swan*, p. 270; *Ape and Essence*, pp. 1ff.

75. *Ape and Essence*, p. 218. The title is an echo of *Measure for Measure* (Act II, scene 2, line 120):

> . . . but man, proud man,
> Drest in a little brief authority,

> Most ignorant of what he's most assured,
> His glassy essence, like an angry ape,
> Plays such fantastic tricks before high heaven
> As makes the angels weep . . .

76. *Point Counter Point*, p. 218.
77. *Ape and Essence*, p. 122.
78. *Ibid.*, p. 148.
79. *Ibid.*, p. 146.
80. *Ibid.*, p. 111.
81. *Island*, p. 264.
82. *The Perennial Philosophy* (New York, 1945), p. 96.
83. *The Genius and the Goddess* (London, 1955), pp. 1, 33.
84. *Ibid.*, p. 40.
85. *Ibid.*, p. 36.
86. *Ibid.*, pp. 26f.
87. *Ibid.*, p. 99.
88. *Ibid.*, pp. 126f.
89. *Ibid.*, p. 86.

Chapter Six

1. "Variations on Goya" appears in *Themes and Variations* (1950). "Breughel" and "Sabbioneta" are included in *Along the Road* (1925).

2. The essay dealing with Prince is entitled "Justifications" and appears in *The Olive Tree* (1936). Maine de Biran is the subject of "Variations on a Philosopher" in *Themes and Variations* (1950). Harriman's story is told in "Ozymandias, the Utopia that Failed." This essay and "Gesualdo: Variations on a Musical Theme" appear in *Tomorrow and Tomorrow and Tomorrow* (1956) (English title: *Adonis and the Alphabet*).

3. "Comfort" appears in the collection of essays entitled *Proper Studies* (1927).

4. *Tomorrow and Tomorrow and Tomorrow* (New York, 1956), pp. 273f.

5. See the long chapter, "The Religious Background" (iii), which interrupts the biographical presentation in *Grey Eminence*. Chap. iii in *The Devils of Loudun* is devoted to a similar inspection of the seventeenth-century forms of religious knowledge and activity.

6. *The Olive Tree*, p. 174.
7. *Grey Eminence*, p. 97.
8. *Ibid.*
9. *The Devils of Loudun*, pp. 167f.
10. *Grey Eminence*, p. 92.
11. *The Devils of Loudun*, pp. 167f.
12. *Ibid.*, pp. 108–80. For a discussion of the phenomena of pos-

session, see Louis Monden, S. J., *Signs and Wonders* (New York, 1966), pp. 164ff.

13. *Ibid.*, pp. 224–62.
14. *Grey Eminence*, pp. 60ff., 77–89.
15. *Ends and Means*, pp. 1ff.
16. *Grey Eminence*, p. 270.
17. *Ibid.*, p. 62.
18. John 14:28.

Chapter Seven

1. *Island* (New York, 1962), p. 4.
2. *Ibid.*, pp. 23, 40.
3. *Ibid.*, p. 84.
4. *Ibid.*, p. 85.
5. *Ibid.*, pp. 41f.
6. *Ibid.*, p. 87.
7. *Proper Studies*, pp. 116–26.
8. *Island*, p. 1. For specific accounts of receptivity, see pp. 35f. and 254f.
9. *Ibid.*, p. 263.
10. *Ibid.*, p. 305.
11. *Ibid.*, p. 185.
12. *Ibid.*, p. 197.
13. *Ibid.*, pp. 105f.
14. *Ibid.*, pp. 218f.
15. *Ibid.*, pp. 333f.
16. *Ibid.*, pp. 49–70.
17. *Ibid.*, pp. 194f.
18. *Ibid.*, pp. 154ff.
19. *Ibid.*, pp. 79f.

Chapter Eight

1. *Jesting Pilate*, p. 57.
2. *The Devils of Loudun*, pp. 74ff.
3. *Tomorrow and Tomorrow and Tomorrow* (New York, 1956), p. 184ff.

Selected Bibliography

The prime bibliographical guide to the study of Aldous Huxley is the following work: *Aldous Huxley, a Bibliography: 1916–1959* by Claire John Eschelbach and Joyce Lee Shober (foreword by Aldous Huxley), Berkeley and Los Angeles, University of California Press, 1961. There is a valuable supplement in the following publication: *Extrapolation: a Science-fiction Newsletter*, Wooster, Ohio, Department of English, The College of Wooster, vol. 6, no. 1: "Aldous Huxley: a Bibliography, 1960–1964", by Thomas D. Clareson and Carolyn S. Andrews.

The information which appears below is drawn chiefly from these two works, although there is some supplementation. The list of Huxley's published books and pamphlets under PRIMARY SOURCES is complete. For a listing of Huxley's uncollected articles and reviews, one should turn to the two bibliographies mentioned above. The list of books about Huxley under SECONDARY SOURCES is selective, as is the annotated sampling of the extensive critical comment on Huxley. No attempt has been made to reproduce the extensive lists of critical comment on individual works which are offered in Eschelbach and Shober, pp. 105–123, and in Clareson and Andrews, pp. 17–20.

PRIMARY SOURCES

The Burning Wheel. Oxford: Blackwell, 1916.
Jonah. Oxford: Holywell Press, 1917.
The Defeat of Youth, and Other Poems. Oxford: Blackwell, 1918.
Leda. London: Chatto and Windus, 1920; New York: Doran, 1920.
Limbo. London: Chatto and Windus, 1920; New York: Doran, 1920.
Crome Yellow. London: Chatto and Windus, 1921; New York: Doran, 1922.
Mortal Coils. London: Chatto and Windus, 1922; New York: Doran, 1922.
Antic Hay. London: Chatto and Windus, 1923; New York: Doran, 1923.

On the Margin, Notes and Essays. London: Chatto and Windus, 1923; New York: Doran, 1923.

Little Mexican. London: Chatto and Windus, 1924; New York: Doran, 1924 (With title *Young Archimedes, and Other Stories*).

Those Barren Leaves. London: Chatto and Windus, 1925; New York: Doran, 1925.

Along the Road, Notes and Essays of a Tourist. London: Chatto and Windus, 1925; New York: Doran, 1925.

Selected Poems. Oxford: Blackwell, 1925; New York: Appleton, 1925.

Essays New and Old. London: Chatto and Windus, 1926; New York: Doran, 1926.

Jesting Pilate. London: Chatto and Windus, 1926; New York: Doran, 1926.

Point Counter Point. London: Chatto and Windus, 1928; New York: Doran, 1928.

Arabia Infelix, and Other Poems. London: Chatto and Windus, 1929; New York: The Fountain Press, 1929.

Do What You Will. London: Chatto and Windus, 1929; Garden City: Doubleday, Doran, 1928.

Holy Face, and Other Essays. London: The Fleuron, 1929.

Appenine. Gaylordsville, Conn.: The Slide Mountain Press, 1930.

Brief Candles. London: Chatto and Windus, 1930; Garden City: Doubleday, Doran, 1930.

Vulgarity in Literature, Digressions from a Theme. London: Chatto and Windus, 1930; Garden City: Doubleday, Doran, 1933.

Music at Night, and Other Essays. London: Chatto and Windus, 1931; Garden City: Doubleday, Doran, 1931.

The Cicadas, and Other Poems. London: Chatto and Windus, 1931; Garden City: Doubleday, Doran, 1931.

The World of Light, a Comedy in Three Acts. London: Chatto and Windus, 1931; Garden City: Doubleday, Doran, 1931.

Brave New World. London: Chatto and Windus, 1932; Garden City: Doubleday, Doran, 1932.

Rotunda, a Selection from the Works of Aldous Huxley. London: Chatto and Windus, 1932.

Texts and Pretexts, an Anthology with Commentaries. London: Chatto and Windus, 1932; New York: Harper, 1933.

T. H. Huxley as a Man of Letters. London: Macmillan, 1932.

The Letters of D. H. Lawrence. Edited and with an introduction by ALDOUS HUXLEY. London: Heinemann, 1932; New York: Viking, 1932.

Retrospect, an Omnibus of Aldous Huxley's Books. Garden City: Doubleday, Doran, 1933.

Beyond the Mexique Bay. London: Chatto and Windus, 1934; New York: Harper, 1934.

1936 . . . Peace? London: Friends Peace Committee, 1936.

Eyeless in Gaza. London: Chatto and Windus, 1934; New York: Harper, 1936.

The Olive Tree, and Other Essays. London: Chatto and Windus, 1936; New York: Harper, 1937.

What Are You Going to Do About It? London: Chatto and Windus, 1936; New York: Harper, 1937.

An Encyclopedia of Pacifism. Edited by ALDOUS HUXLEY. London: Chatto and Windus, 1937; New York: Harper, 1937.

Ends and Means, an Enquiry into the Nature of Ideals and into the Methods Employed for Their Realization. London: Chatto and Windus, 1937; New York: Harper, 1937.

The Elder Peter Bruegel. With an essay by ALDOUS HUXLEY and a note by JEAN VIDEPOCHE (pseudonym for HERBERT M. ALEXANDER). New York: Wiley Book Company, 1938.

The Most Agreeable Vice. Los Angeles: Ward Ritchie Press, 1938.

After Many a Summer Dies the Swan. London: Chatto and Windus, 1939; New York: Harper, 1939.

Words and Their Meanings. Los Angeles: Ward Ritchie Press, 1940.

Grey Eminence, a Study in Religion and Politics. London: Chatto and Windus, 1941; New York: Harper, 1941.

The Art of Seeing. London: Chatto and Windus, 1943; New York: Harper, 1942.

Time Must Have a Stop. London: Chatto and Windus, 1945; New York: Harper, 1944.

Twice Seven, Fourteen Selected Stories. London: Reprint Society, 1944.

The Perennial Philosophy. London: Chatto and Windus, 1946; New York: Harper, 1945.

Verses and a Comedy. London: Chatto and Windus, 1946.

Collected Short Stories. London: Chatto and Windus, 1957; New York: Harper, 1957.

Brave New World Revisited. London: Chatto and Windus, 1958; New York: Harper, 1958.

Collected Essays. New York: Harper, 1959.

On Art and Artists. Edited by MORRIS PHILIPSON. London: Chatto and Windus, 1960; New York: Harper, 1960.

Island. London: Chatto and Windus, 1962; New York: Harper, 1962.

Literature and Science. London: Chatto and Windus, 1963; New York: Harper and Row, 1963.

SECONDARY SOURCES

1. *Books about Aldous Huxley*

ATKINS, JOHN A. *Aldous Huxley: a Literary Study.* London: Calder, 1956. Represents an enthusiastic acceptance of Huxley's claims to represent a valid reaction to the problems of his time. Attention centers on the novels as vehicles of Huxley's chief ideas.

GHOSE, SISIRJUMAR. *Aldous Huxley: a Cynical Salvationist.* New York: Asia Publishing House, 1962. Traces with clarity the development of Huxley's intellectual position, with highly useful analyses of Huxley's relation with Eastern thought.

HEINTZ-FRIEDRICH, SUZANNE. *Aldous Huxley: Entwicklung seiner Metaphysik.* Lugano: Veladini, 1948. Contains a full account of Huxley's development, from his early period of negative analysis to the period of *The Perennial Philosophy*, which is analyzed as a kind of terminus of his entire intellectual development.

HENDERSON, ALEXANDER. *Aldous Huxley.* London: Chatto and Windus, 1935. Represents a conviction that Huxley has been a central figure in the intellectual struggles of his time.

POSCHMANN, WILHELM. *Das Kritische Weltbild bei Aldous Huxley.* Düsseldorf: Dissertations Verlag, 1937. Useful analysis of the interplay of idea and influence in Huxley's earlier work.

VANN, GERALD, O. P. *On Being Human: St. Thomas and Mr. Aldous Huxley.* Studies Huxley's early work from a Thomistic point of view and argues that Huxley is concerned with something like the fullness and interdependency of experience that St. Thomas described.

2. *Selected Comments in Books and Periodicals*

ADCOCK, A. ST. JOHN. *The Glory that was Grub Street.* London: Sampson, Low, n.d. Interesting as an early reaction to Huxley; great emphasis on Huxley's presentation of sex.

ALLEN, WALTER. *Tradition and Dream.* London: Phoenix House, 1964. Brief but just summary of Huxley's career; esteem for Huxley's early work and a fair recognition of the difficulties of the mystical insight for a novelist.

BEACH, JOSEPH WARREN. "Counterpoint: Aldous Huxley." *The Twentieth Century Novel: Studies in Technique.* New York: Century, 1932. Centers attention on Huxley's techniques and possible artistic antecedents.

BROOKE, JOCELYN. "The Wicked Uncle: an Appreciation of Aldous Huxley," *Listener*, LXX (December 12, 1963), 99. Testimony to Huxley's influence.

BUCK, PHILO M. "Sight to the Blind: Aldous Huxley." *Directions in Contemporary Literature.* New York: Oxford, 1942. Regards Huxley's novels as the pursuit of freedom in an oppressive world and approves the emergence of mystical insight.

BURGUM, EDWIN B. "Aldous Huxley and His Dying Swan." *The Novel and the World's Dilemma.* New York: Oxford, 1947. Contains a most vigorous attack on Huxley's defects of social vision and political commitment.

CHASE, RICHARD. "The Huxley-Heard Paradise," *Partisan Review,* X (March–April, 1943), 143–58. Reasoned and hostile attack on the views shared by Huxley and Heard; their works represent a retreat from the reality of the human situation.

CHESTERTON, GILBERT K. "End of the Moderns." *The Common Man.* New York: Sheed and Ward, 1950. Charitable estimate of Huxley and Lawrence as representatives of a revolution that has reached its conclusion.

CHURCH, MARGARET. "Aldous Huxley's Attitude Toward Duration." *College English,* XVII (April, 1956), 388–91. Argues that Huxley's attitude toward time creates discontinuity in human experience.

CONNOLLY, CYRIL. *Enemies of Promise and Other Essays.* Garden City: Doubleday, 1960. Useful analysis of "Mandarin prose," the elaborate style habitual with Huxley.

DAICHES, DAVID. "Aldous Huxley." *The Novel and the Modern World.* Chicago: University of Chicago Press, 1939. Sees the bitterness of Huxley's fiction as an expression of disappointed romanticism; stresses the essay quality in all of Huxley's work.

DYSON, A. E. "Aldous Huxley and the Two Nothings," *Critical Quarterly,* III (Winter, 1961), 78–84. Sees Huxley's struggles between the two "nothings" of the flesh and the infinite as admirable, if artistically unsatisfactory.

ELIOT, T. S. "Le roman anglais contemporain," *Nouvelle revue francais* (May 1, 1927), p. 674f. Curt remarks on "la religion chic" that threatens Huxley in *Those Barren Leaves.*

GLICKSBERG, CHARLES I. "Aldous Huxley: Arts and Mysticism," *Prairie Schooner,* XXVII (Winter, 1953), 344–53. Sympathetic account of Huxley's movement forward from the Waste Land of *Antic Hay.*

HACKER, A. "Dostoyevsky's Disciples: Man and Sheep in Political Theory," *Journal of Politics,* XVII (November, 1955), 590–613. Brief, pointed discussion of *Brave New World* that sees the novel as a record of the failure of liberal autonomy.

HALL, JAMES. "The Appeal to Grandfathers: Aldous Huxley." *The Tragic Comedians: Seven Modern British Novelists,* Bloomington, Ind.: Indiana University Press, 1963. Stresses the importance of

Huxley's early work as a model for the novels of other writers; particularly concerned with the efforts of characters in *Antic Hay* to create a personal myth.

HEARD, GERALD. "The Poignant Prophet," *Kenyon Review*, XXVII (Winter, 1965), 49–70. Full account of Heard's relationship with Huxley; interesting indications about the origin of the later work.

HENDERSON, PHILIP. *The Novel Today*. London: John Lane, 1936. Asserts that emotional immaturity lay beneath the cultured skepticism of the early novels.

HOFFMAN, CHARLES G. "The Change in Huxley's Approach to the Novel of Ideas," *Personalist*, XLII (1961), 85–90. Censures Huxley's later novels as works in which one set of ideas is given the advantage over opposing conceptions.

HOFFMAN, FREDERICK JOHN. "Aldous Huxley and the Novel of Ideas." *Forms of Modern Fiction: Essays Collected in Honor of Joseph Warren Beach*. Ed. WILLIAM VAN O'CONNOR. Minneapolis: University of Minnesota Press, 1948. Discusses Huxley's novels of ideas as the proper expression of an unstable age; judges that the later novels represent a failure to preserve a necessary detachment.

"Huxley Brothers," *Life*, XXII (March 24, 1947), 53ff. Interesting set of photographs.

JOAD, CYRIL E. M. *Return to Philosophy*. London: Faber and Faber, 1935. Employs Huxley, throughout the book, as one of the chief examples of modern man's failure to respect and use reason.

KARL, F. R. and MAGALANER, M. "Aldous Huxley." *A Reader's Guide to Great Twentieth Century Novels*. New York: Noonday, 1959. Presents Huxley as a novelist of ideas which are poorly realized in the characters and actions of the novels; underlines the representative value of Huxley for the twentieth century.

KESSLER, MARTIN. "Power and the Perfect State: a Study of Disillusionment as Reflected in Orwell's *Nineteen Eighty-four* and Huxley's *Brave New World*," *Political Science Quarterly*, LXXII (December, 1957), 565–77. Respectful analysis of the sociological import of the two utopias.

LA ROCHELLE, D. "A propos d'un roman anglais," *Nouvelle revue francais*, XIX (November, 1930), 721–31. Essay on *Point Counter Point* which finds the novel a masterly exposition of the results of moral and social disintegration.

MACCARTHY, DESMOND. "Poetry of Aldous Huxley," *Living Age*, CCCVII (October 9, 1920), 107–11. Early estimate of the worth of Huxley's poetry.

MATSON, FLOYD W. "Aldous and Heaven Too: Religion among the Intellectuals," *Antioch Review*, XIV (September, 1954), 293–309.

Sympathetic view of Huxley's career as representative of the testing of various alternatives in the twentieth century.

MAUROIS, ANDRÉ. "Aldous Huxley." *Prophets and Poets*. New York: Harper, 1935. Admiringly underlines Huxley's erudition and his ability to embrace many features of his time; sees dangers, however, in Huxley's excessive intellectualism.

MULLER, HERBERT JOSEPH. "Apostles of the Lost Generation: Huxley and Hemingway." *Modern Fiction: a Study of Values*. New York: Funk and Wagnalls, 1937. Regards *Eyeless in Gaza* as the successful emergence of a sense of social responsibility in a writer who suffers from a tendency to amuse and condescend.

NAGARAJAN, S. "Religion in Three Recent Novels of Aldous Huxley," *Modern Fiction Studies*, V (Summer, 1959), 153–65. Highly useful discussion of the relations of religious insight and fiction in Huxley's work; judges that Huxley's avoidance of Christian insight is disenabling.

NICHOLSON, NORMAN. "Aldous Huxley and the Mystics," *Fortnightly*, n.s. CLXVII (February, 1947), 131–35. Sees continuity in the growth of Huxley and regards him as a modern Gnostic; censures Huxley's treatment of the mysticism of the West.

QUINA, JAMES H. "The Philosophical Phases of Aldous Huxley," *College English*, XXIII (May, 1962), 636–41. Judges that Huxley's changes of interest are realizations of problems set in the early novels rather than cancellations.

ROBERT, JOHN H. "Huxley and Lawrence," *Virginia Quarterly Review*, XIII (Autumn, 1937), 546–57. Recognizes the importance of Lawrence as a mentor to Huxley and remains skeptical as to the mystical insight to resolve Huxley's intellectual problems.

SAVAGE, DEREK S. "Aldous Huxley and the Dissociation of Personality." *The Withered Branch, Six Studies in the Modern Novel*. New York: Pellegrini and Cudahy, 1952. Sees Huxley's total work as a kind of autobiography expressive of unfolding concepts which the novels attempt to dramatize; regards *The Perennial Philosophy* as the key to this development.

SCHALL, J. V. "Buber and Huxley: Recent developments in Philosophy," *Month*, XIX (February, 1958), 97–102. Contrasts the attitudes of Huxley and Buber toward language as a means of human communication. Huxley's suspicions of language are justifiable but need not represent a terminal estimate.

SPENCER, THEODORE. "Aldous Huxley: the Latest Phase," *Atlantic Monthly*, CLXV (March, 1940), 407–9. Sees Huxley as a very apt spokesman for his generation, and *After Many a Summer Dies the Swan* as a move toward positive and constructive assertion.

TINDALL, WILLIAM YORK. *Forces in Modern British Literature.* New York: Knopf, 1947. Brief but informative notes on the two phases of Huxley's career.

————. "The Trouble with Aldous Huxley," *American Scholar,* XI (Autumn, 1942), 452–64. Regards Huxley's later career as a decline from early successes; in addition, Tindall judges that the influence of Gerald Heard is responsible for a religiosity that is artistically damaging and otherwise deleterious.

WAUGH, EVELYN, ANGUS WILSON, FRANCIS WYNDHAM, JOHN WAIN, and PETER QUENNEL. "A Critical Symposium on Aldous Huxley," *London Magazine,* II (August, 1955), 51–64. Particularly valuable as testimony to the impact of Huxley's work on younger men. Wain (p. 58) characterizes Huxley as a writer of tracts and a hater of ordinary human experience.

WEBSTER, H. T. "Aldous Huxley: Notes on a Moral Evolution," *South Atlantic Quarterly,* XLV (July, 1946), 372–83. Stresses the element of continuity in Huxley's development.

WILSON, COLIN. "Existential Criticism and the Work of Aldous Huxley," *London Magazine,* V (September, 1958), 46–59. Somewhat sympathetic study that finds Huxley's shortcomings the result of an avoidance of the experience of existing. Wilson regards *The Perennial Philosophy* as a valuable introduction to mystical thought.

ZAEHNER, R. C. "Mescalin and Aldous Huxley," *Listener,* LV (April 26, 1956), 506f. Stern remarks on Huxley's use and hasty interpretation of the mescalin experience; particularly objects to Huxley's failure to discriminate among types of mysticism.

Index